Round The World Cookbook

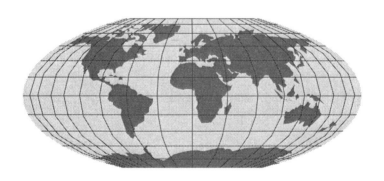

Recipes & Party Ideas

Great American Opportunities, Inc./Favorite Recipes® Press

President: Thomas F. McDow III
Editorial Manager: Mary Jane Blount
Editors: Georgia Brazil,
Mary Cummings, Jane Hinshaw,
Linda Jones, Mary Wilson
Typography: Jessie Anglin,
Sara Anglin, Pam Newsome

Published by:
Favorite Recipes® Press, a division of
Great American Opportunities, Inc.
P. O. Box 305142
Nashville, Tennessee 37230

Manufactured in the United States of America
First Printing: 1993   25,000 copies
Second Printing: 1993   12,000 copies

Library of Congress Number: 92-44405
ISBN: 0-87197-362-6

Table of Contents

Globe-Trotting for Stay-at-Homes

*A*sk any world traveler about his or her adventures and food is one of the first things mentioned. Even the most everyday foods of a foreign land may seem unlikely, exciting or exotic to those of us raised on hamburgers, tuna casseroles and fried chicken, but you may be surprised to find that your "All-American" diet has already introduced you to round-the-world cuisine.

Have you eaten an English muffin or Spanish rice? Could you enjoy a crisp tossed salad without French or Italian salad dressing? And what about Swedish meatballs, Canadian bacon and Swiss steak?

Spaghetti may be Italian to almost everyone, but did you know that the Chinese invented pasta? If the Earl of Sandwich invented meat between bread slices, how did pita pockets, stuffed baguettes and rolled up tortillas become the same kind of pickup meal?

Is your kitchen equipped with such necessities as a Dutch oven and a French chef's knife? Does your pantry include Greek olives, Polish sausage, curry powder, French-style green beans and Parmesan cheese? If your airplane flight includes dinner, do you know what to expect if you opt for Chicken Kiev or Lasagna?

If you were asked to recommend a good restaurant to someone searching for couscous, would you suggest a Chinese restaurant? Could you peruse the menu of a good Italian restaurant and feel confident that you were not ordering the proprietor? Would you order calimari, escargot or brioche for a wonderful sweet bread to accompany your Viennese or Turkish coffee or China tea?

Let us help you scan the horizon in the comfort of your home, learn a bit about the tastes of the world, and some of the vocabulary that will make you seem the seasoned traveler.

For you students of a foreign language, we have even provided some French, German, Italian and Spanish translations of a few recipes. If you have been fortunate enough to study more than one of those languages, you may find it interesting to compare them as we have presented several recipes in the English version (suitable for anyone to cook by) as well as in each of the four languages mentioned above. If Latin is your language, you will find it enlightening to compare the languages which have roots in the Latin. Even if foreign languages hold no appeal at all, this cookbook will be a welcome addition to your kitchen as your taste buds call for something different—or maybe not as different as you may think.

What's in a Name?

*A*s Mr. Shakespeare once inquired. Does it matter that a pastry in English is an *empañada* in Spanish or that a *quiche* has the crust on the bottom and the *knoedel* is on the top? What if the cover is made of cornmeal or phyllo? We all know a pie when we eat one whether it is small and individual or just a piece of a big one. Shakespeare also said, "There is nothing new under the sun," but with only a bit of imagination and a few hints along the way you should be able to see the similarities among the following "pie" recipes. You will even see the first example of one recipe in five versions—English, French, German, Italian and Spanish. Throughout this cookbook you can have the fun of discovering favorite foods in new costumes and soon-to-be favorites that added to your cooking repertoire will make you the envy of your less well traveled friends.

Asparagus Pie

(English Version)

1 recipe 1-crust pie pastry
2 pounds fresh asparagus, cooked
1³/₄ cups cream
5 eggs
Salt, pepper and paprika to taste

*L*ine pie plate with pie pastry. Prick with fork; weight down with dried beans. Bake at 350 degrees for 20 minutes or until lightly browned. Cut asparagus into 2-inch pieces. Place in prepared pie crust. Beat cream, eggs, salt and pepper in bowl. Pour over asparagus. Sprinkle with paprika. Bake at 400 degrees for 15 minutes or until set. Yield: 6 servings.

Tourte Argenteuil

(French Translation)

Pâte brisée
32 onces de petites asperges cuites
1³/₄ tasses de crème fraîche
5 œufs
Sel, poivre, paprika

Foncez un moule de pâte. Piquez et parsemez de quelques haricot secs. Mettez à four chaude une vingtaine de minutes. Retirez lorsque la pâte commence à se colorer. Coupez les asperges en tronçons de 4 centimètres. Battez la crème avec les œufs et assaisonnez avec du sel et du poivre. Nappez les asperges avec la crème. Saupoudrez de paprika. Faites cuire 15 minutes à four chaud à 400 degrés. Pour 6 personnes.

Spargel Quiche

(German Translation)

1 Pastetenteig ausreichend für eine Quiche
2 Pfund frischer Spargel, gekocht
1³/₄ Tassen süße Sahne
5 Eier
Salz, Pfeffer und Paprika nach Geschmack

Kuchenform mit Pastetenteig auslegen. Den Teig mit einer Gabel einstechen; mit getrockneten Bohnen zum Niederdrücken auffüllen. 20 Minuten bei 350 Grad Fahrenheit oder bis leicht gebräunt backen. Den Spargel in 5cm große Stücke schneiden. In die vorbereitete Teigkruste geben. Sahne, Eier, Salz und Pfeffer in einer Schüssel schlagen. Über den Spargel gießen. Paprika darüberstreuen. Bei 400 Grad Fahrenheit 15 Minuten lang oder bis zum Setzen backen. Für 6 Personen.

Tortino d'Asparagi

(Italian Translation)

1 ricetta di pasta da tortino
2 libbre d'asparagi freschi, cotti
1³/₄ tazze panna
5 uova
Sale, pepe e paprica a piacere

Mettere la pasta nella tortiera. Pungerla con una forchetta; coprire con un pezzo di carta oleata. Metterci qualche fave asciutta per appesantirla. Cuocere a 350 gradi 20 minuti o finché un po' dorata. Tagliare gli asparagi in pezzi di 2 pollici di lunghezza. Metterli nella pasta preparata. Mescolare la panna, le uova, il sale ed il pepe in una ciotola. Versare sugli asparagi. Spargere il tutto con la paprica. Cuocere a 400 gradi 15 minuti o finché solido. Porzioni: 6.

Pastel de espárrago

(Spanish Translation)

1 pastel para tarta (o sea, la parte empanada de una tarta)
de tamaño de 9 pulgadas
2 libras de espárrago
1³/₄ tazas de nata no batida
5 huevos
sal, pimienta y paprika a gusto

Forrar una fuente para tartas con el pastel para tarta. Hacer agujeros en el pastel con un tenedor; llenar de frijoles secos para sujetar la masa, cocinar al horno a 350 grados por 20 minutos, o hasta que se dore un poco. Cortar el espárrago en trozos de 2 pulgadas. Meter el espárrago en el pastel ya preparado. Batir en una fuente la nata, los huevos, la sal y la pimienta. Echarse esta mezcla al espárrago. Rociar con un poco de paprika. Cocinar al horno a 400 grados por 15 minutos, o hasta que se cuaje. Rendimiento: 6 porciones.

Greek Ground Beef Pie

1 package frozen phyllo dough
1½ pounds lean ground beef   3 potatoes, peeled, shredded
2 cups sliced fresh mushrooms   2 tomatoes, chopped
1 onion, chopped   1 cup chopped parsley
1½ teaspoons allspice
½ teaspoon garlic powder   1 teaspoon salt
½ teaspoon pepper   ¾ cup melted margarine
Grated Parmesan cheese

Let phyllo dough stand in refrigerator for 12 hours. Let stand, unopened, for 2 to 4 hours at room temperature. Brown ground beef in skillet, stirring until crumbly; drain. Add potatoes, mushrooms, tomatoes, onion, parsley, allspice, garlic powder, salt and pepper; mix well. Simmer, covered, for 20 to 30 minutes or until liquid is nearly absorbed, stirring frequently. Cut phyllo dough into twelve 8x12-inch sheets; cover with towel to prevent drying out. Brush 8x12-inch baking dish with margarine. Layer 6 sheets of dough in dish, brushing each sheet with melted margarine. Spoon ground beef mixture into prepared dish. Top with remaining 6 sheets dough, brushing each sheet with margarine. Bake at 350 degrees for 30 minutes or until golden brown. Sprinkle with cheese. Yield: 8 servings.

German Sauerkraut and Knoedel

1 onion, chopped   1 teaspoon butter
1 pound sauerkraut, drained, rinsed   2 cups water
1½ pounds Hungarian or Polish sausage
1 envelope dry yeast   1 cup warm milk
1 teaspoon sugar   1 egg   1 teaspoon salt
2 cups flour   1 tablespoon melted butter

Sauté onion in 1 teaspoon butter in saucepan. Add sauerkraut, water and sausage. Simmer for 1 hour. Dissolve yeast in milk in bowl. Add sugar, egg and salt; mix well. Mix in flour. Let rise in bowl for 30 to 45 minutes or until doubled in bulk. Invert dough onto simmering sauerkraut. Simmer, covered, for 30 minutes; do not remove cover during cooking time. Remove to serving plate; drizzle knoedel with 1 tablespoon melted butter. Cut into wedges to serve. Yield: 4 servings.

Italian Spinach and Sausage Pie in Cornmeal Pastry

12 ounces sausage
1/2 cup chopped mushrooms
2 10-ounce packages frozen chopped spinach, thawed
2 eggs
24 ounces cottage cheese, drained
1/2 cup chopped onion
2 tablespoons flour
1 1/2 cups shredded mozzarella cheese
1/3 cup grated Parmesan cheese
Cornmeal Pastry
1 egg, slightly beaten

Brown sausage with mushrooms in skillet, stirring frequently; drain. Squeeze spinach to remove moisture. Beat 2 eggs and cottage cheese in mixer bowl until smooth. Add sausage mixture, spinach, onion, flour and cheeses; mix well. Spoon into 9-inch pie plate lined with Cornmeal Pastry. Top with remaining pastry. Brush with 1 egg. Bake at 425 degrees on lower oven rack for 15 minutes. Reduce oven temperature to 350 degrees. Bake for 35 to 40 minutes longer or until brown. Let stand for 10 minutes. Yield: 6 servings.

Cornmeal Pastry

2 cups flour
1/2 cup white cornmeal
1/4 cup grated Parmesan cheese
1/2 teaspoon salt
3/4 cup butter
6 to 8 tablespoons cold water

Mix flour, cornmeal, cheese and salt in bowl. Cut in butter until mixture forms coarse crumbs. Stir in enough water to form dough. Chill in refrigerator. Roll into 2 circles on floured surface. Yield: 2 pie shells.

Mexican Empañadas

2/3 cup finely chopped onion
1 cup finely chopped celery
1 pound ground beef   1   3-ounce jar mushrooms
1 cup finely chopped stuffed olives
1   8-ounce can tomato paste
1/2 teaspoon oregano
Salt and pepper to taste
3 packages pie crust mix
2 cups shredded Cheddar cheese

Sauté onion and celery in skillet sprayed with nonstick cooking spray for 8 minutes. Add ground beef. Cook until ground beef is brown and crumbly, stirring constantly; drain. Add mushrooms, olives, tomato paste, oregano, salt and pepper; mix well. Prepare pie crust mix using package directions. Roll dough very thin on floured surface. Cut into 2 1/2 to 3-inch rounds. Spoon ground beef filling onto rounds; sprinkle with cheese. Moisten edges; fold dough over to enclose filling and seal with fork. Place on baking sheet. Bake at 400 degrees for 18 to 20 minutes or until light brown. Yield: 80 servings.

Cornish Pasties

4   12-ounce short crust pastries
12 ounces lean steak, cut into small pieces
4 ounces potato, finely chopped
1 onion, finely chopped
Salt and pepper to taste   1 carrot, finely chopped
1 turnip, finely chopped
2 teaspoons margarine

Roll pastry into four 8-inch rounds on floured surface. Combine steak, potato, onion, salt, pepper, carrot and turnip in bowl; mix well. Add 1/4 of the mixture to each pastry. Dampen edge of pastry with water; fold to form half a circle. Press edges to seal; cut vent. Place 1/2 teaspoon margarine in vent. Place in 8-inch round baking pans. Bake at 400 degrees for 20 minutes. Reduce temperature to 350 degrees. Bake on middle rack for 40 minutes longer. May be served hot or cold. Yield: 4 servings.

French Tourtière

This is a savory pork pie from France.

1 onion, chopped
1/2 clove of garlic, crushed
2 tablespoons bacon drippings
1 1/2 pounds ground pork
3/4 cup broth or bouillon
1 teaspoon salt
1/4 teaspoon pepper
Mace, savory and/or sage to taste
2 tablespoons chopped parsley
1 recipe 2-crust pie pastry
2 tablespoons cream

Sauté onion and garlic in bacon drippings in saucepan until light brown. Add ground pork. Cook until light brown, stirring until crumbly; drain. Stir in broth, salt and pepper. Cook for 10 minutes or until liquid is nearly absorbed. Add mace, savory, sage and parsley. Cool to room temperature. Spoon into pastry-line 9-inch deep-dish pie plate. Top with remaining pastry; seal edges and cut vents. Brush with cream. Bake at 425 degrees for 20 minutes. Reduce oven temperature to 350 degrees. Bake for 20 to 30 minutes longer or until golden brown. Serve warm or cold. Yield: 6 servings.

Now that you have the idea—crusts of pie pastry, phyllo dough, yeast dough—think of the many other possibilities—biscuit dough, puff pastry dough, roll dough or a batter the filling can nestle into. Happy—and adventurous—eating!

What in the World's for Supper?

A nodding acquaintance with the following terms should make your introduction to a new culinary experience a smidge less surprising and more enjoyable.

French

Au gratin—describes a dish sprinkled with bread crumbs or cheese, and then baked.

Béchamel—basic white sauce made with milk or stock.

Bisque—a cream soup made with shellfish or puréed vegetables.

Brioche—a slightly sweet bread usually served at breakfast.

Coquille—literally, a shell; it refers to seafood dishes prepared in scallop shells or baking dishes in the shape of a shell. The best known dish is Coquilles St. Jacques, made with scallops.

Crêpe—thin pancake, filled with sweet or savory mixtures, often served flaming or with a sauce.

Croutons—small cubes of bread, often seasoned, served with soups or as garnish for salad if desired.

Quiche—main dish one-crust pastry with savory custard filling.

Ratatouille—a casserole or stew usually containing eggplant, zucchini, tomato and green pepper. It can include meat as well.

Soufflé—a savory or sweet dish made with beaten eggs and baked until puffed.

Indian/Pakistani

Chutney—a highly seasoned relish of fruits, herbs and spices.

Curry—any dish, including meat, fish, vegetables or fruit seasoned with curry powder.

Poori—fried bread usually shaped as small thin rounds.

Italian

Al dente—describes pasta which has been cooked just to the point at which it still offers a slight resistance to the teeth.

Antipasto—appetizers, or dishes served "before the pasta."

Lasagna—a layered dish made with wide noodles, a sauce made with or without meat and cheese.

Minestrone—a soup made of fresh vegetables, dried beans and at least one type of pasta.

Pasta—literally paste; it refers to noodle-like dough, either fresh or dried, which comes in over 100 different shapes and varieties such as spaghetti, macaroni, canneloni and rotini.

Pesto—a green sauce made of basil, garlic, Parmesan cheese and pine nuts. It is served over pasta.

Pomodoro—a tomato.

Tortoni—a frozen dessert made with whipped cream, macaroon crumbs and liqueur.

Zabaglione—a dessert made of eggs, sugar and wine. It can be served warm or cold, alone or over fruit or cake.

Chinese

Bean curd—also called tofu, cheeselike product made from soybean milk.

Cantonese—in the style of northern China distinguished by lighter flavors and seasonings.

Five spices—a blend of equal amounts of cinnamon, ginger, anise, fennel and cloves.

Hoisin sauce—thick seasoning made from beans, sugar and spices.

Oyster sauce—made from oysters but not fishy tasting.

Szechwan—Chinese province featuring fiery spices.

German

Kuchen—means "cake" but not rich and sweet so much as a base for rich toppings of streusel or fruit.

Sauer—the sour of typically German sweet and sour dishes such as sauerbraten and sauerkraut.

Schnitzle—a thin cutlet of pork or veal.

Spätzle—a very small dumpling made of flour.

Wurst—sausage of many varieties such as bratwurst.

Greek

Avgolemono—a soup or sauce made from chicken stock, eggs and lemon juice.

Baklava—a dessert made of very thin sheets of pastry filled with nuts and honey, then baked and cut into diamond shapes.

Feta—soft white cheese made from the milk of goats or sheep and cured in brine.

Moussaka—dish made of eggplant, onion and spices. It usually contains ground lamb as well.

Phyllo—tissue-thin layers of flaky pastry. The layers can be filled with sweet or savory mixture and served as appetizer, main dish or dessert.

Pilaf—rice dish which can include various combinations of meat, vegetables and seasonings. It can be served as a main dish or side dish.

Middle Eastern

Bulgur—parched and crushed wheat used as a dietary staple in Middle Eastern countries.

Lentils—one of the oldest known legumes. Its flat seeds are always used dried and prepared like dried peas or beans.

Shish kabob—pieces of meat and vegetables threaded onto skewers and broiled.

Tahini—paste of sesame seed.

Yogurt—a milk product made acidic and thickened by the addition of bacterial cultures. It is a dietary staple in the Middle Eastern countries where it may be made from goat's milk or camel's milk.

Russian and Polish

Borscht—soup of beets, cabbage and meat usually garnished with sour cream.

Kolaches—sweet yeast rolls filled with jam that are frequently made in small size and served like cookies.

Spanish/Latin American

Arroz—any form of rice.

Chalupas—a spicy dish made with tortillas layered or filled with meat sauce and cheese.

Empañada—pastry filled with sweet or savory mixture. Frequently they take the form of turnovers and can be baked or fried.

Enchilada—rolled tortilla filled with meat or cheese and topped with chili sauce.

Flan—a baked dessert custard.

Gazpacho—a cold soup made with tomatoes and other fresh vegetables that have been finely chopped.

Jalapeño pepper—very hot small green pepper.

Paella—national dish of rice and any combination of seafood, chicken, sausage, vegetables and seasonings.

Salsa—a sauce containing tomatoes and green chili peppers.

Seviche—appetizer or main dish of raw fish pickled or marinated in lime juice and mixed with onions and peppers.

Tortilla—the national bread of Mexico; it is a thin flat cake made of cornmeal or flour and baked on a griddle.

Main Dishes

Japanese Pike Tempura with Ginger Dipping Sauce

1½ pounds walleye pike filets
¼ cup cornstarch
¾ cup flour   ½ cup cornstarch
1 tablespoon salt
1 tablespoon baking powder
1 cup water   3 cups peanut oil
Ginger Dipping Sauce

Remove and discard skin from filets; cut into ½x3-inch strips. Coat with ¼ cup cornstarch. Mix flour, ½ cup cornstarch, salt and baking powder in large bowl. Whisk in water gradually until smooth. Heat oil to 350 degrees in large skillet. Dip several fish strips at a time into batter; shake off excess batter, leaving light coating. Place fish strips in hot oil. Fish should rise to surface immediately; if it does not the oil is not hot enough. Fry for 2 to 3 minutes or until golden brown. Drain on triple layer of paper towels for 2 to 3 minutes. Arrange fried fish strips in bowl lined with absorbent paper. Serve with Ginger Dipping Sauce. May substitute any firm white-fleshed fish for pike. This is also an excellent appetizer. Yield: 3 to 4 servings.

Ginger Dipping Sauce

½ cup soy sauce
2 tablespoons rice wine vinegar or white wine vinegar
2 tablespoons sugar   Hot pepper sauce to taste
1 tablespoon freshly minced gingerroot
2 teaspoons thinly sliced scallion

Combine soy sauce, vinegar, sugar and hot sauce in small bowl; stir until sugar dissolves. Stir in gingerroot and scallion. Set aside to allow flavors to develop. Yield: ¾ cup.

Photograph for these recipes is on previous page.

Next to beef steak, roast beef and beef stew, stroganoff is probably the most popular family beef recipe. It is easy, tasty and nourishing. The ingredients are good basic items for refrigerator and pantry. But were you surprised to learn that stroganoff has its roots in Russia? Sour cream in soups, gravies and sauces is almost a necessity in Russian and Hungarian dishes.

Easy Beef Stroganoff

(English Version)

1¹/₂ pounds lean beef, cubed
Flour for dredging
1 teaspoon garlic powder
¹/₂ cup chopped onion
3 tablespoons shortening
2 10-ounce cans beef bouillon
1 cup sliced mushrooms
8 ounces sour cream

Dredge beef in flour. Brown beef, garlic powder and onion in hot shortening in saucepan, stirring frequently. Add bouillon. Simmer for 30 to 60 minutes or until beef is tender, stirring frequently. Add mushrooms and sour cream. Cook until heated through; do not boil. Serve over rice or noodles.
Yield: 4 to 5 servings.

Bœuf Stroganoff

(French Translation)

1¹/2 livres de bœuf, coupé en morceaux
Farine   1 cuillerée à café d'ail en poudre
¹/2 tasse d'oignon haché
3 cuillerées à soupe de saindoux
2 boîtes de 10 onces de bouillon de viande
1 tasse de champignons émincés
8 onces de crème aigre

Saupoudrez les morceaux de bœuf avec de la farine. Faites-les bien revenir avec l'ail en poudre' les oignons hachés et le saindoux dans une poêle. Versez le bouillon dans la poêle. Mijotez sur un feu doux pendant 30 minutes à 1 heure, jusqu'à ce que les morceaux de bœuf soient tendres, en les remuant souvent. Ajoutez les champignons et la crème. Laissez cuire quelques minutes mais sans bouillir. Servez avec des nouilles ou du riz. Pour 4 à 5 personnes.

Leichtzuzubereitendes Rind Stroganoff

(German Translation)

1¹/2 Pfund mageres Rindfleisch, gewürfelt
Mehl   1 Teelöffel Knoblauchpulver
¹/2 Tasse gewürfelte Zwiebeln   3 Eßlöffel Fett
2 Dosen à 10 Unzen Rinderbrühe
1 Tasse blättrig geschnittene Champignons
8 Unzen saure Sahne

Die Rindfleischwürfel in Mehl wenden. Rindfleisch, Knoblauchpulver und Zwiebel in dem heißen Fett in einem Saucentopf unter häufigem Umrühren anbräunen. Brühe hinzufügen. Bei schwacher Hitze 30 Minuten bis zu einer Stunde oder bis das Rindfleisch zart ist unter häufigem Umrühren kochen lassen. Die Champignons und die saure Sahne hinzufügen. Bis kurz vor dem Aufkochen erhitzen, aber nicht zum Kochen bringen. Über Reis oder Nudeln anrichten. Für 4 oder 5 Personen.

Individual Beef Wellingtons

*This elegant dish is a small version of the **English** recipe which presents a whole cooked beef filet in a puff pastry crust.*

2 cups chopped fresh mushrooms
1/4 cup margarine   1 tablespoon sherry
4   1-inch filet mignon steaks
1/4 cup margarine
1   8-count can crescent rolls

Cook mushrooms in 1/4 cup margarine and sherry in skillet until liquid is nearly absorbed. Brown steaks lightly on both sides in 1/4 cup margarine in large skillet. Separate roll dough into 4 squares, pressing diagonal perforations to seal. Place spoonful of mushrooms on each square; top with steak. Bring up corners of dough to enclose steak, pressing edges to seal. Place mushroom side up on baking sheet. Bake at 425 degrees for 8 to 10 minutes or until golden brown. May broil for several minutes if necessary to complete browning. Yield: 4 servings.

Chinese Pepper Steak

1 tablespoon cornstarch
1/2 teaspoon sugar   1/4 teaspoon ginger
1/4 cup soy sauce   1 pound beef round steak
2 tablespoons oil
2 medium green bell peppers, cut into 1-inch pieces
1 clove of garlic, minced
1/4 cup water
2 small tomatoes, cut into wedges

Mix cornstarch, sugar and ginger in bowl. Stir in soy sauce. Cut steak into thin strips. Add to soy sauce mixture. Stir-fry 1/3 at a time in hot oil in 10-inch skillet until brown; remove to warm platter. Reduce heat. Add green peppers, garlic and water. Stir-fry for 5 to 6 minutes or until green peppers are tender-crisp. Stir in beef and tomatoes. Cook until heated through. Serve over rice. Yield: 4 servings.

Korean Marinated Beef

2 pounds sirloin tip, very thinly sliced
2 pounds onions, sliced into thin rings
1 6-ounce bottle of soy sauce
¹/₄ cup sugar
1 teaspoon red pepper
2 tablespoons oil

Place sirloin in shallow glass dish. Combine onions, soy sauce, sugar and red pepper in bowl; mix well. Pour over beef. Marinate for 30 minutes or longer. Stir-fry in hot oil in wok or skillet just until beef is no longer pink. Serve over rice or rice noodles. Yield: 6 servings.

Rouladen

*These **German** steak rolls have a surprise filling.*

4 ¹/₄-inch thick 4-ounce round steaks
2 tablespoons Dijon mustard
1 dill pickle, sliced into thin strips
4 slices bacon, cut into halves
¹/₄ cup chopped onion
¹/₄ cup oil
2 cups boiling water
4 bouillon cubes
¹/₂ teaspoon tomato paste
3 tablespoons cornstarch
1 cup sour cream

Spread steaks with mustard. Place 1 pickle strip at narrow end of each steak. Place 2 pieces bacon on each steak. Sprinkle with onion. Roll to enclose filling; tuck in sides and secure with wooden picks. Brown in oil in skillet. Add water, bouillon cubes and tomato paste. Simmer, covered, for 1¹/₂ to 2 hours or until tender. Remove steak rolls to serving platter; remove picks. Add mixture of cornstarch and sour cream to skillet; mix well. Cook just until thickened, stirring constantly; do not boil. Pour over steak rolls. Yield: 4 servings.

Boboti

*An interesting combination of dried fruits and spices with ground beef, this **African** dish is a cousin of Greek Moussaka.*

2 medium onions, sliced   2 teaspoons margarine
2 pounds lean ground beef   1 egg
1/4 cup milk   2 slices white bread, cubed
1/4 cup chopped dried apricots
1/4 cup dark raisins   2 tablespoons sugar
1 tablespoon curry powder
2 tablespoons lemon juice   2 teaspoons salt
1/4 teaspoon pepper   5 bay leaves
2 eggs   3/4 cup milk   1/4 teaspoon turmeric

Sauté onions in margarine in skillet until golden brown. Add ground beef. Cook until brown, stirring frequently; drain. Combine 1 egg, 1/4 cup milk and bread cubes in large bowl; mix well. Add next 7 ingredients; mix well. Add ground beef mixture; mix gently. Spoon mixture into 2-quart baking dish; place bay leaves on top. Bake at 350 degrees for 30 minutes. Remove bay leaves. Beat remaining 2 eggs with remaining 3/4 cup milk in small bowl. Add turmeric, stirring until just blended. Pour over casserole. Bake for 10 to 12 minutes longer or until topping is set. Serve with rice and chutney. Yield: 8 to 10 servings.

Oriental Burgers

*Hamburgers visit the **Far East**.*

1 pound ground beef   1 medium onion, chopped
1   16-ounce can bean sprouts, drained
1   8-ounce can sliced water chestnuts
1/3 cup soy sauce   1/3 cup water
1 tablespoon molasses   2 tablespoons cornstarch
2 tablespoons water   Salt to taste   Sesame seed buns

Brown ground beef with onion in skillet, stirring frequently; drain. Add next 5 ingredients; mix well. Cook over medium heat for 5 minutes. Stir in mixture of cornstarch and remaining 2 tablespoons water. Bring to a boil. Simmer for 1 minute. Season with salt. Serve on warm, toasted sesame seed buns. Yield: 8 servings.

German Sauerbraten Meatballs

Meatballs with gingersnap sauce.

1 pound ground beef   1 egg   ³/₄ cup soft bread crumbs
¹/₄ cup water   ¹/₄ cup chopped onion
¹/₂ teaspoon salt   1¹/₂ cups water
2 beef bouillon cubes
¹/₃ cup packed light brown sugar   ¹/₄ cup dark raisins
2¹/₂ tablespoons lemon juice
¹/₂ cup coarsely crumbled gingersnaps

Combine ground beef with egg, bread crumbs, ¹/₄ cup water, onion and salt in bowl; mix well. Shape into 1-inch balls. Bring 1¹/₂ cups water to a boil in saucepan. Stir in bouillon cubes, brown sugar, raisins, lemon juice and gingersnap crumbs. Add meatballs. Simmer for 10 minutes. Turn over meatballs and baste with sauce. Simmer for 10 minutes longer. Yield: 6 servings.

Köttbullar

*Serve these **Swedish** meatballs for dinner or make tiny ones to serve as appetizers.*

2 cups soft bread crumbs   ²/₃ cup milk
¹/₂ cup minced onion   1 tablespoon butter
1¹/₂ pounds ground beef   3 eggs, slightly beaten
¹/₂ teaspoon nutmeg   ¹/₂ teaspoon allspice
2 teaspoons salt   ¹/₂ teaspoon pepper
3 tablespoons butter   2 tablespoons flour
1 cup (about) milk

Soak bread crumbs in ²/₃ cup milk in bowl. Sauté onion in 1 tablespoon butter in small skillet for 3 minutes. Add onion to softened bread crumbs in bowl. Add ground beef, eggs, nutmeg, allspice, salt and pepper; mix well. Shape into small balls. Brown on all sides in remaining 3 tablespoons butter in large skillet. Remove to bowl. Stir flour into drippings in skillet. Add 1 cup milk gradually. Cook until thickened, stirring constantly. Add meatballs. Simmer for 10 minutes. May substitute sour cream for milk, adding 1 tablespoon at a time until gravy is of desired consistency. May substitute ground veal for beef. Yield: 10 servings.

Fatiar

*These **Lebanese** meat pies are similar to chimichangas.*

**2 envelopes dry yeast   2¹/2 cups warm water
7 cups (about) flour   1 tablespoon sugar
1 tablespoon salt   2 pounds lean ground beef
2 small onions, chopped   Juice of 3 lemons
2 teaspoons salt   ¹/2 teaspoon pepper
¹/2 teaspoon allspice   ¹/2 cup oil**

Dissolve yeast in 1 cup warm water in large bowl. Add remaining 1¹/2 cups water, 6 cups flour, sugar and salt; mix well. Add enough remaining 1 cup flour to make moderately stiff dough. Knead on floured surface for 10 minutes or until smooth and elastic. Place in greased bowl, turning to coat surface. Let rise, covered, until doubled in bulk. Brown ground beef with onions in skillet, stirring frequently; drain and cool. Stir in lemon juice and seasonings. Punch dough down. Shape into small balls. Roll each ball into 5-inch circle. Spoon ¹/4 cup ground beef mixture into center of each circle. Fold dough to center; pinch to seal and make 3-cornered tart. Pour oil into deep baking sheet. Place meat pies on baking sheet. Bake at 350 degrees for 25 minutes or until brown.
Yield: 16 servings.

Pasty Pie

*A large version of **English** pasties.*

**Pastry for 2-crust pie
2¹/2 cups thinly sliced potatoes
1 thinly sliced onion
1 pound lean ground beef
1¹/2 teaspoons salt   ¹/8 teaspoon pepper
2 tablespoons melted margarine**

Line deep baking dish with half the pastry. Layer potatoes, onion, ground beef, salt, pepper and margarine alternately in pastry. Top with remaining pastry. Seal pastry tightly to retain steam and juice. Bake at 375 degrees for 1 hour. Yield: 6 servings.

Chimichangas

*Fried beef pies with a **Latin American** twist.*

6 large flour tortillas
3 cups Beef for Chimichangas
Vegetable oil for frying
Shredded lettuce
1 7-ounce can green chili salsa
2 tomatoes, chopped
1 cup sour cream

Warm tortillas in 350-degree oven for 5 minutes. Warm Beef for Chimichangas in small saucepan. Spread ½ cup beef mixture on lower ⅓ of each tortilla. Fold bottom edge over filling. Fold both sides toward center; roll as for jelly roll. Secure with a pick. Fry in 400-degree oil in electric skillet for 2 minutes or until golden and crisp. Drain on paper towels. Serve on shredded lettuce; top with green chili salsa, tomatoes and sour cream.
Yield: 6 servings.

Beef for Chimichangas

1 5-pound beef roast
1 tablespoon vegetable shortening
1 onion, chopped
1 4-ounce can chopped green chilies
2 7-ounce cans green chili salsa
¼ teaspoon garlic powder
¼ cup flour   4 teaspoons salt
1 teaspoon ground cumin

Place roast in deep baking pan. Do not add salt or water. Bake, tightly covered, at 200 degrees for 12 hours or until well done. Drain, reserving liquid. Let roast stand until cool. Remove bones; shred meat. Melt shortening in large skillet. Add onion and green chilies. Sauté for 1 minute. Add chili salsa, garlic powder, flour, salt and cumin. Cook for 1 minute over medium-low heat. Stir in reserved pan liquid and shredded meat. Cook for 5 minutes or until slightly thickened. Let stand until cool. May freeze.
Yield: 30 servings.

Moussaka

*A traditional **Greek** casserole.*

2 eggplant
1/2 cup shortening
2 tablespoons butter
4 medium onions, chopped
3 cloves of garlic, chopped
1 pound ground lamb
1/2 teaspoon thyme
1/2 teaspoon oregano
1/2 cup canned tomatoes
1 teaspoon salt   2 egg whites
1/2 cup bread crumbs
2 tablespoons flour
2 tablespoons melted butter
1 1/2 cups milk
1/2 teaspoon salt   2 egg yolks
1/4 teaspoon nutmeg
4 teaspoons Parmesan cheese

Cut eggplant into slices lengthwise. Brown on both sides in short-ening in skillet; remove to platter. Add 2 tablespoons butter, onions and garlic in skillet. Sauté just until wilted. Stir in ground lamb, thyme, oregano, tomatoes and 1 teaspoon salt. Simmer, covered, for 30 minutes. Let stand until cool. Stir in unbeaten egg whites and half the crumbs. Sprinkle remaining crumbs into greased baking dish. Layer eggplant and lamb mixture 1/2 at a time in prepared dish. Blend flour and 2 tablespoons melted butter in saucepan. Stir in milk and 1/2 teaspoon salt. Cook over low heat until smooth and thickened, stirring constantly. Stir a small amount of hot mixture into egg yolks; stir egg yolks into hot mixture. Season with nutmeg. Pour over layers in baking dish. Sprinkle with cheese. Bake at 350 degrees for 1 hour. Yield: 8 servings.

Kibbi

*These are **Middle Eastern** pocket sandwiches.*

¹/₂ cup bulgur wheat
1 medium onion, ground
1 pound ground lamb   1 teaspoon salt
¹/₈ teaspoon pepper
¹/₄ teaspoon allspice
Butter or margarine
Pocket Bread

Wash bulgur wheat. Soak in water for 2 hours or until soft; drain. Combine wheat, ground onion, ground lamb, salt, pepper and allspice in large bowl; mix well. Press mixture firmly into 8x8-inch baking pan. Score into triangles. Dot each triangle with butter. Bake at 375 degrees for 45 minutes. Serve with Pocket Bread. Yield: 4 to 5 servings.

Pocket Bread

1 envelope dry yeast
1¹/₃ cups warm water
1 teaspoon salt
1 tablespoon vegetable or olive oil
¹/₄ teaspoon sugar   3¹/₂ cups flour   Cornmeal

Dissolve yeast in warm water in large mixer bowl. Stir in salt, oil, sugar and 1¹/₂ cups flour. Beat until smooth. Stir in enough remaining flour to make dough easy to handle. Turn onto lightly floured surface. Knead for 10 minutes or until dough is smooth and elastic. Place in greased bowl, turning to grease surface. Let rise, covered, in warm place for 1 hour. Dough is ready if an indentation remains when touched. Punch dough down. Divide into 12 equal portions; shape into balls. Let rise for 30 minutes. Sprinkle 3 ungreased baking sheets with cornmeal. Flatten each ball into ¹/₈-inch thick circle. Place on prepared baking sheets. Let rise for 30 minutes. Bake at 500 degrees for 10 minutes or until loaves are puffed and light brown. Remove from baking sheet; cool on wire rack. Yield: 12 servings.

Shish Kabob

*This **Middle Eastern** meal on-a-skewer should be
served while sizzling hot.*

1 large onion, finely chopped
2 tablespoons olive oil
3 tablespoons lemon juice
1½ teaspoons thyme   Salt and pepper to taste
2 pounds 1-inch lamb cubes
Cherry tomatoes   Mushrooms
Green bell peppers, cut into pieces

Combine onion, oil, lemon juice, thyme salt and pepper in bowl. Add lamb. Marinate in refrigerator for 6 hours to overnight; drain. Alternate lamb cubes with tomatoes, mushrooms and green peppers on skewers. Grill to desired degree of doneness. Yield: 6 servings.

Greek Lamb Stew

2 to 2½ pounds lamb shoulder
2 tablespoons olive oil
1 onion, chopped
2 tablespoons olive oil
2 or 3 cloves of garlic, minced
1 pound fresh or frozen green beans, cut into 2-inch pieces
3 or 4 tomatoes, peeled, chopped
4 to 6 cups water   1 tablespoon rosemary
1 tablespoon oregano
Salt and pepper to taste

Trim fat from lamb; cut lamb into 1-inch cubes. Brown in 2 tablespoons olive oil in heavy saucepan over medium-high heat. Sauté onion in 2 tablespoons olive oil in skillet until translucent. Add garlic. Sauté until tender. Add onions and garlic to lamb. Add green beans, tomatoes, 4 cups water, rosemary, oregano, salt and pepper. Simmer for 3 hours, adding additional water if needed for desired consistency. May also add okra if desired. Yield: 6 servings.

Shepherd's Pie

*A favorite pie on the menu of every **English** pub.*

1 pound finely chopped lamb
1 medium onion, finely chopped
1 cup beef stock   Salt and pepper to taste
3 tablespoons cornstarch
1 pound potatoes, cooked
2 tablespoons butter   ½ cup (about) milk

Sauté lamb with onion in saucepan until tender. Stir in beef stock. Simmer for 30 minutes, skimming fat as needed. Season with salt and pepper. Stir in mixture of cornstarch and a small amount of water. Cook for 3 minutes or until thickened, stirring constantly. Spoon into baking dish. Mash potatoes with butter and milk in bowl. Spoon carefully over top of pie. Bake at 350 degrees for 30 minutes or until brown. Yield: 6 servings.

German Meats and Sauerkraut

6 bratwurst
1 kielbasa sausage, cut into 2-inch pieces
6 onions, peeled, cut into halves crosswise
6 smoked pork chops
4 ounces unsliced bacon
3 pounds sauerkraut, rinsed, drained
2 green apples, chopped
1 red bell pepper, chopped   6 peppercorns
1 tablespoon caraway seed
1 tablespoon paprika
3 cups light nonalcoholic beer

Brown bratwurst, kielbasa and onions in skillet; drain. Layer pork chops, bacon, bratwurst mixture, sauerkraut, apples and red pepper in saucepan. Add peppercorns, caraway seed and paprika. Pour beer gently over all. Simmer for 1 hour. Remove peppercorns. Serve with green beans, dark bread and German white wine. Add parsley-buttered noodles or potatoes for a heartier dinner. Yield: 6 to 8 servings.

Sausage-Apple Sauerkraut

*This is a **German** version of Shepherd's Pie.*

1 pound sausage
2 tablespoons chopped onion
1 apple, peeled, sliced
2 cups sauerkraut
1/2 teaspoon caraway seed
2 cups mashed potatoes
1/3 cup shredded Cheddar cheese
Paprika to taste

Brown sausage in skillet; drain, reserving 2 tablespoons drippings. Sauté onion in reserved drippings. Layer sausage, onion, apple and sauerkraut in deep-dish pie plate. Sprinkle with caraway seed. Spread potatoes over top. Sprinkle with cheese and paprika. Bake at 350 degrees for 35 minutes or until golden brown. Yield: 6 servings.

Calzone

***Italian** sausage rolls are hearty enough for a main dish or great with pasta and salad.*

1 loaf frozen bread dough, thawed
1 pound unseasoned pork sausage
1 pound lean ground beef   2 tablespoons fennel seed
Salt and pepper to taste   Olive oil
Dry Romano cheese   Oregano to taste

Let bread dough rise until tripled in bulk. Brown sausage and ground beef with fennel seed, salt and pepper in skillet, stirring until coarsely crumbled; drain in colander. Cool. Roll out dough on oiled board into two 1/4-inch thick rectangles. Spread with sausage-beef mixture. Roll as for jelly roll from wide end. Brush with olive oil; sprinkle with cheese and oregano. Place on lightly greased baking pan. Bake at 375 degrees for 20 to 25 minutes or until golden brown. Yield: 8 to 10 servings.

French Filet de Porc Normande

1 tablespoon oil   1 tablespoon butter
1 2-pound boned pork loin, rolled, tied   2 onions, sliced
3 tart apples, peeled, sliced
3 tablespoons apple juice concentrate   1 tablespoon flour
1½ cups chicken stock   Salt and pepper to taste
⅓ cup whipping cream   2 tablespoons butter
2 apples, unpeeled, cut into ⅜-inch slices
2 tablespoons sugar

Heat oil and 1 tablespoon butter in Dutch oven. Brown pork on all sides over medium-high heat. Remove from pan. Add onions. Cook until soft but not brown. Add peeled apple slices. Cook until apples and onions are golden brown. Return pork to pan. Pour apple juice concentrate over pork. Stir flour, chicken stock, salt and pepper into pan juices. Bring to a boil, stirring constantly. Place in oven. Bake, covered, at 350 degrees for 1½ to 2 hours or until tender. Remove pork from pan to warm plate. Strain pan juices into saucepan, mashing apples. Bring to a boil. Cook until thickened. Add cream. Bring to a boil, stirring constantly. Add salt and pepper. Spoon over pork. Heat 2 tablespoons butter in skillet. Dip 1 side of unpeeled apple slices in sugar. Arrange sugar side down in butter. Cook over high heat for 4 to 5 minutes or until caramelized. Sprinkle remaining sugar over apples; turn. Cook for 4 to 5 minutes longer. Arrange apple slices over pork. Yield: 6 to 8 servings.

Italian Sausage Fettucini

12 ounces cream   8 to 10 mushrooms, sliced
1 clove of garlic, minced   1 egg yolk, beaten
1 12-ounce package fettucini, cooked
1 pound bulk hot Italian sausage, cooked, drained
¾ cup Parmesan cheese

Combine cream, mushrooms and garlic in saucepan. Simmer over low heat until mushrooms are tender. Add a small amount of hot mixture to egg yolk; stir egg yolk into hot mixture. Cook over low heat until thickened, stirring constantly. Place fettucini in warmed serving bowl. Add sausage, cheese and sauce; toss to mix. Yield: 6 servings.

Frankfurters Paprikash

*In **Austria**, paprika is more than a red sprinkle*
for color on deviled eggs.

1 cup minced onion   2 tablespoons butter or margarine
1 teaspoon vegetable oil   1 cup hot water
1 beef bouillon cube   1 large green bell pepper, chopped
4 teaspoons paprika   8 frankfurters
Dillseed and caraway seed to taste   1/4 teaspoon salt
1/8 teaspoon pepper   2 medium tomatoes, chopped

Sauté onion in butter and oil in large skillet. Add hot water, bouillon cube, green pepper and paprika. Simmer for 3 to 4 minutes. Add frankfurters, dillseed, caraway seed, salt and pepper. Simmer for 8 to 10 minutes. Stir in tomatoes. Cook for 2 minutes longer. Serve with rice, buttered noodles or mashed potatoes. Garnish with green pepper rings. Yield: 4 servings.

German Fruit-Stuffed
Pork Loin Roast

3/4 cup chopped prunes   3/4 cup chopped dried apricots
1 tablespoon grated gingerroot   1 teaspoon grated orange rind
1/2 teaspoon cinnamon   1/2 teaspoon cumin
Salt and pepper to taste   1   4-pound pork loin roast
2 teaspoons cider vinegar   1/4 cup packed light brown sugar
2 teaspoons flour   1 teaspoon dry mustard
1 teaspoon cumin   1/2 cup water   1 teaspoon cornstarch

Combine first 8 ingredients in bowl; mix well. Split roast lengthwise, leaving 1 side intact. Spoon fruit mixture into roast; secure halves with string. Place in roasting pan. Spread mixture of next 5 ingredients over roast. Bake at 325 degrees for 1 1/2 hours or until cooked through, basting occasionally with pan juices. Remove roast to warm platter. Skim grease from pan juices. Add 1/2 cup water to roasting pan, stirring to deglaze. Stir in mixture of cornstarch and a small amount of cold water. Cook on stove top for 1 minute or until thickened to desired consistency, stirring occasionally. May strain if desired. Serve with roast. Yield: 8 servings.

Kung Pao Pork

Far Eastern stir-fries are great with pork too!

1 pound pork tenderloin   1 tablespoon soy sauce
1¹/₂ tablespoons cornstarch   1¹/₂ tablespoons cold water
1¹/₂ tablespoons sugar   1¹/₂ teaspoons vinegar
1 teaspoon cornstarch   1 teaspoon sesame oil
2 tablespoons (or more) peanut oil
2 to 5 dried red peppers   1 teaspoon chopped fresh ginger
¹/₂ cup salted peanuts

Slice pork into ¹/₂-inch strips. Combine with soy sauce, 1¹/₂ tablespoons cornstarch and water in bowl; mix well. Marinate for 20 minutes. Mix sugar, vinegar, 1 teaspoon cornstarch and sesame oil in bowl; set aside. Heat 1 tablespoon peanut oil in hot wok or large skillet. Add pork mixture. Stir-fry until cooked through. Remove pork to warm platter. Add 1 tablespoon peanut oil and red peppers. Stir-fry for several seconds. Remove and discard peppers. Add ginger, pork and peanuts. Stir-fry for several seconds. Stir in vinegar mixture. Cook until thickened, stirring constantly. Serve over rice or chow mein noodles. Yield: 4 servings.

Mandarin Pork Stir-Fry

2 tablespoons cornstarch   1¹/₄ cups water   ¹/₃ cup soy sauce
¹/₃ cup corn syrup   ¹/₃ to ¹/₂ teaspoon crushed dried red pepper
1 pound pork tenderloin   2 cloves of garlic, minced
4 tablespoons oil   2 cups chopped broccoli
2 onions, thinly sliced   2 carrots, cut into 2-inch strips
1 7-ounce can water chestnuts, cut into halves or quarters
8 ounces mushrooms   1 cup rice, cooked

Blend cornstarch and water in bowl. Stir in next 3 ingredients; set aside. Cut pork into thin strips. Stir-fry with garlic in 2 tablespoons oil in large skillet or wok for 5 minutes or until tender. Remove from skillet. Heat remaining 2 tablespoons oil in skillet. Add broccoli, onions and carrots. Stir-fry for 3 minutes. Add water chestnuts and mushrooms. Stir-fry for 1 minute or until vegetables are tender-crisp. Return pork to skillet. Stir in cornstarch mixture. Cook for 1 minute or until thickened to desired consistency, stirring constantly. Serve over rice. Yield: 6 servings.

Oktoberfest German Sauerkraut

A German pot roast.

4   32-ounce jars sauerkraut, rinsed, drained
3 apples, peeled, cut into wedges
2 large baking potatoes, cubed
1 pound bacon, cut into 1-inch pieces
1   3-pound pork loin tip roast, trimmed, cubed
1 large onion, chopped
2 to 4 cups water
Caraway seed to taste

Place sauerkraut in electric roaster. Add apple wedges and potato cubes. Sauté bacon in skillet sprayed with nonstick cooking spray; drain, reserving pan drippings. Add bacon to sauerkraut. Sauté cubed pork and onion in reserved pan drippings. Add to sauerkraut; mix well. Stir in 2 cups water. Cook, covered, in electric roaster at 250 degrees for 1 hour. Add caraway seed. Cook for 7 hours longer, adding water as needed to prevent scorching. Yield: 20 servings.

Oriental Pork Chops

1/3 cup soy sauce
1/4 cup oil
1/4 cup orange juice
1/4 cup chopped green bell pepper
1 tablespoon brown sugar
2 teaspoons ginger
1 teaspoon turmeric
6   1 1/2-inch pork chops

Combine soy sauce, oil, orange juice, green pepper, brown sugar, ginger and turmeric in bowl; mix well. Arrange pork chops in shallow dish. Add marinade. Marinate, covered, in refrigerator for 3 hours to overnight, turning occasionally. Drain, reserving marinade. Place on grill over low coals and hickory chips. Grill for 25 minutes on each side, basting occasionally with reserved marinade. May broil if preferred. Yield: 6 servings.

Pork Schnitzel

*A **German** pork version of a veal favorite.*

6 pork tenderloin cutlets   ¹/₄ cup flour
1 teaspoon seasoned salt
¹/₄ teaspoon pepper   1 egg, beaten
2 teaspoons milk   ³/₄ cup dry bread crumbs
1 teaspoon paprika
1 tablespoon shortening   ³/₄ cup chicken broth
1 teaspoon flour   ¹/₂ cup sour cream
¹/₄ teaspoon dillweed

Pound pork ¹/₈ to ¹/₄ inch thick with meat mallet. Cut small slits in edges. Coat with mixture of ¹/₄ cup flour, seasoned salt and pepper. Dip in mixture of egg and milk. Coat with mixture of bread crumbs and paprika. Cook 3 cutlets at a time in shortening in large skillet for 2 to 3 minutes on each side. Remove to warm platter. Add broth to skillet, stirring to deglaze. Stir in 1 teaspoon flour, sour cream and dillweed. Cook until thickened, stirring constantly; do not boil. Serve with cutlets. Yield: 6 servings.

Cazuela de Puerco

*A **Spanish** pork stew.*

2 pounds boneless pork, cut into ¹/₂-inch cubes
1 cup chopped onions   1 clove of garlic, minced
¹/₄ cup olive oil   1¹/₂ cups uncooked rice
³/₄ cup finely chopped green bell pepper
1 20-ounce can tomatoes   2¹/₂ cups beef broth
1¹/₂ teaspoons salt
¹/₂ cup chopped stuffed olives

Trim fat from pork. Sauté onions and garlic in hot oil in skillet until onions are tender. Remove onions to bowl. Add pork to pan drippings in skillet. Cook over medium heat for 10 minutes. Combine pork, onions, rice, green peppers, tomatoes, beef broth and salt in greased 1¹/₂-quart casserole. Bake, covered, at 325 degrees for 50 minutes, adding a small amount of boiling water if necessary. Add olives. Bake for 5 minutes longer. Yield: 6 servings.

Try this easy all-in-one dish for breakfast, brunch or even supper. Add some eggs on the side if you insist but the pub keeper may not approve. For breakfast buffets the guests will be delighted by your response when they ask, "What do you call this?"

Toad-in-the-Hole

(English Version)

1 pound small link pork sausages
1 cup milk
2 eggs
1 cup flour
1 tablespoon melted butter
¹/₂ teaspoon salt

Fry sausages in skillet until light brown on all sides; drain. Place in 9x9-inch baking pan. Combine milk, eggs, flour, butter and salt in blender container. Process for 1 minute or until smooth. Pour over sausages. Bake at 375 degrees for 30 minutes or until topping is puffed and golden brown. Yield: 6 servings.

Grenouille-au-Trou

(French Translation)

1 livre de petites saucisses de porc
1 tasse de lait
2 œufs
1 tasse de farine
1 cuillerée à soupe de beurre fondu
1/2 cuillerée à café de sel

Faites revenir les saucisses dans une poêle au feu moyen jusqu'à ce qu'elles soient dorées, en les retournant de temps en temps; égouttez-les. Mettez-les dans un plat allant au four. Mélangez le lait, les œufs, la farine, le beurre et le sel dans un mixer pendant 1 minute pour obtenir une pâte homogène. Versez la pâte sur les saucisses. Mettez à cuire au four à 375 degrés pendant 30 minutes ou jusqu'à ce que la pâte soit gonflée et bien dorée.
Pour 6 personnes.

Wurst in Kuchenteig

(German Translation)

1 Pfund kleine Schweinswürstchen
1 Tasse Milch
2 Eier
1 Tasse Mehl
1 Eßlöffel zerlassene Butter
1/2 Teelöffel Salz

Würstchen in der Pfanne von allen Seiten anbraten, bis sie gebräunt sind; abtropfen lassen. In eine etwa 25x25 cm große Bratform geben. Milch, Eier, Mehl, Butter und Salz in den Mixbehälter geben; eine Minute lang oder bis die Masse gut verrührt ist mixen. Über die Würstchen gießen. Bei 375 Grad Fahrenheit 30 Minuten lang, oder bis der Belag aufgebläht und goldbraun ist, backen. Für 6 Personen.

Rospo nel buco

(Italian Translation)

1 libbra salsicce piccole
1 tazza latte
2 uova
1 tazza farina
1 cucchiaio burro sciolto
¹/₂ cucchiaino sale

Friggere le salsicce in una padella finché marroni su tutti i lati; scolare. Mettere in una casseruola di 9 x 9 pollici. Mescolare insieme il latte, le uova, la farina, il burro e il sale in frullatoio; far girare per un minuto o finché omogeneo. Versare sulle salsicce. Cuocere al forno a 375 gradi per 30 minuti o finché sia rosolato e alto. Porzioni: 6.

Sapo-en-el-hoyo

(Spanish Translation)

1 libra de salchichas pequeñas de puerco
1 taza de leche
2 huevos
1 taza de harina
1 cucharada de mantequilla derretida
¹/₂ cucharadita de sal

Freír las salchichas en una sartén hasta que estén totalmente doradas; quitar la grasa derretida. Meter en una cacerola de 9 por 9 pulgadas. Combinar la leche, los huevos, la harina, la mantequilla y la sal en una batidora; mezclar por 1 minuto, o hasta que esté sin grumos. Echar la mezcla a las salchichas. Cocinar al horno a 375 grados por 30 minutos, o hasta que la superficie esté inflada y dorada. Rendimiento: 6 porciones.

Vietnamese Pork Brochette

Oriental shish kabob—don't forget to soak the wooden skewers.

1 green onion, chopped   1 tablespoon pepper
1 tablespoon salt   6 to 8 tablespoons fish sauce
2 teaspoons garlic powder
3 tablespoons sugar   3 pounds pork tenderloin
1 onion   1 green bell pepper   13 wooden skewers

Combine first 6 ingredients in bowl; mix well. Cut pork into 1-inch cubes. Cut onion and green pepper into wedges. Marinate pork, onion and green pepper in prepared sauce for at least 2 hours. Soak wooden skewers in water for 30 minutes. Thread pieces of pork, onion and green pepper alternately on skewers. Broil for 5 minutes on 1 side; turn. Broil for 2 minutes longer. Serve with rice or Chinese noodles. Yield: 13 servings.

Chinese Hot and Sour Spareribs

1/4 cup minced green onions   2 cloves of garlic, minced
1 large piece fresh ginger, 1/2 inch thick, chopped
1/4 cup peanut oil
2 pounds country-style spareribs, cut into 1 1/2-inch pieces
1 teaspoon salt   3 tablespoons sugar
3 tablespoons dry sherry
2 tablespoons reduced-sodium soy sauce
2 tablespoons hoisen sauce   2 tablespoons chili pepper oil
2 tablespoons red wine vinegar
1/2 teaspoon pepper   1 cup chicken broth
2 tablespoons chopped fresh cilantro

Sauté green onions, garlic and ginger in peanut oil in Dutch oven for 3 minutes. Rub ribs with salt. Add to Dutch oven. Cook for 8 minutes or until brown on all sides. Add mixture of sugar, sherry, soy sauce, hoisen sauce, chili pepper oil, vinegar and pepper. Cook for 5 minutes. Add chicken broth. Simmer, covered, for 20 minutes. Simmer, uncovered, for 10 minutes longer. Bake at 375 degrees for 1 hour. Transfer to serving plate. Sprinkle with cilantro.
Yield: 4 servings.

English Veal Medallions

12 to 16 ounces boneless veal, cut into 3-inch slices
2 tablespoons butter   1 cup whipping cream
2 teaspoons grated fresh horseradish
1 medium tomato, peeled, seeded, diced
2 teaspoons chopped parsley
2 teaspoons chopped chives
Salt and pepper to taste

Pound veal with mallet to ½-inch thickness. Brown lightly in butter in skillet, turning once. Remove to hot platter. Drain drippings. Add whipping cream and horseradish to skillet. Cook over medium heat for 5 minutes or until mixture is reduced by half, stirring occasionally. Stir in tomato, parsley and chives. Cook for 2 minutes. Season with salt and pepper to taste. Spoon over veal. Yield: 2 servings.

Italian Veal Parmigiana

6 veal cutlets   2 eggs, beaten
¼ teaspoon salt   ⅛ teaspoon pepper
1 cup Italian bread crumbs
1 large onion, chopped   1 clove of garlic, minced
2 tablespoons margarine
2 large green bell peppers, chopped
2 tablespoons margarine   1 15-ounce can tomato sauce
2 cups shredded mozzarella cheese
¼ cup grated Parmesan cheese

Tenderize veal cutlets with meat mallet. Beat eggs with salt and pepper in bowl. Dip cutlets in egg mixture; coat with bread crumbs, reserving remaining crumbs. Sauté onion and garlic in 2 tablespoons margarine in large skillet for 3 minutes. Add green peppers. Sauté for 3 minutes longer. Remove to bowl. Add remaining 2 tablespoons margarine and veal to skillet. Brown for 3 minutes on each side. Place in 9x13-inch baking dish. Top with green pepper mixture. Pour tomato sauce over top; sprinkle with cheeses and reserved bread crumbs. Bake, covered, with foil, at 375 degrees for 40 minutes. Bake, uncovered, for 10 minutes longer. Yield: 6 servings.

Italian Veal Scallopini

1/2 cup flour   1 teaspoon salt
1/4 teaspoon pepper
1/4 teaspoon oregano
1/4 teaspoon garlic powder
1 pound thinly sliced veal
1/4 cup vegetable oil
2 tablespoons butter
1 medium onion, chopped
2 cloves of garlic, minced   1 cup sliced mushrooms
2 teaspoons chopped parsley
1 teaspoon salt   1/4 teaspoon pepper
1/4 teaspoon oregano
3 tomatoes

Combine flour, 1 teaspoon salt, 1/4 teaspoon pepper, 1/4 teaspoon oregano and garlic powder in small bowl. Cut veal into 2-inch pieces. Coat well with flour mixture. Sauté veal in mixture of oil and butter in large skillet until golden brown on both sides. Remove to platter. Add onion and garlic to skillet. Sauté until transparent. Add mushrooms, parsley, 1 teaspoon salt, 1/4 teaspoon pepper and 1/4 teaspoon oregano; mix well. Squeeze tomatoes into mushroom mixture. Add veal. Cook over medium heat until veal is tender, stirring frequently. Yield: 4 servings.

German Wiener Schnitzel

1 1/2 pounds veal steak, 1/2 inch thick
1 teaspoon salt   1/4 teaspoon pepper
4 tablespoons flour   1 egg, lightly beaten
1 tablespoon salad oil   1 cup bread crumbs
1/4 cup butter

Trim and cut veal into 4 pieces; pound thin. Season with salt and pepper. Coat with flour. Dip in mixture of egg and salad oil. Dip in bread crumbs. Chill for 1 hour. Melt butter in skillet over medium heat. Add veal. Brown for 15 minutes on each side or until crisp. Garnish with parsley and lemon wedges. Yield: 4 servings.

Hungarian Goulash

Here's that wonderful paprika again.

3 pounds boneless veal, cut into 1¹/₂-inch cubes
4 cups onion wedges
2 teaspoons salt
2 teaspoons pepper
2 tablespoons Hungarian paprika
1 cup (about) water
4 cups buttered noodles
1 cup sour cream

Combine veal, onions, salt, pepper and paprika in heavy kettle; do not add water. Cook, covered, over medium heat for 20 minutes, stirring frequently. Simmer, covered, for 2 hours or until tender. Add enough water to make gravy of desired consistency. Spoon over buttered noodles. Top with sour cream. Serve with German rye bread. Yield: 6 servings.

Cacciatore

*Nothing common about this easy **Italian** chicken stew.*

3 chicken breasts
1 small onion, chopped
1 green bell pepper, chopped
¹/₂ cup sugar
1 46-ounce can tomato juice
1 15-ounce can Italian tomato sauce
1 6-ounce can Italian tomato paste
1 6-ounce can water
1 tablespoon garlic powder

Cook chicken in water to cover in saucepan for 30 minutes or until tender. Cut chicken into bite-sized pieces. Combine with onion, green pepper, sugar, tomato juice, tomato sauce, tomato paste, water and garlic powder in saucepan. Cook over medium heat for 45 to 50 minutes or to desired consistency. Serve over cooked noodles. Yield: 6 to 8 servings.

Creamy Chicken Crêpes

(French)

1¹/₃ cups flour   1 teaspoon salt   4 eggs, beaten
2 tablespoons vegetable oil
1¹/₃ cups milk   ¹/₂ cup sour cream
1 10-ounce can cream of mushroom soup
2¹/₂ cups chopped cooked chicken
Mushroom Sauce
1 cup shredded Cheddar cheese
Paprika to taste

Combine flour, salt and eggs in bowl; mix well. Add 2 tablespoons oil and milk; beat until smooth. Refrigerate for 2 hours or longer. Brush bottom of 10-inch crêpe pan with oil. Pour 3 tablespoons batter into pan; tilt pan in all directions so that batter covers pan in thin film. Cook over medium heat for 1 minute. Turn crêpe. Cook for 30 seconds. Remove crêpe from pan. Repeat procedure with remaining batter. Set aside 10 crêpes. Freeze remaining crêpes for another purpose. Combine sour cream and soup in bowl; mix well. Add chicken; mix well. Spoon ¹/₃ cup chicken filling into center of each crêpe; roll up. Place seam side down in greased 9x13-inch baking dish. Spoon Mushroom Sauce over crêpes. Bake at 350 degrees for 15 minutes. Sprinkle cheese over crêpes. Bake for 10 minutes. Sprinkle with paprika. Yield: 10 crêpes.

Mushroom Sauce

1 small onion, finely chopped
2 tablespoons butter or margarine
1 chicken bouillon cube   2 tablespoons water
1 2¹/₂-ounce jar sliced mushrooms, drained
¹/₄ cup white grape juice
1 10-ounce can cream of mushroom soup
¹/₂ cup sour cream

Sauté onion in butter in skillet until tender. Add bouillon cube, water and mushrooms. Cook until bouillon cube dissolves, stirring frequently. Add grape juice. Cook until mixture is reduced by ¹/₃. Stir in soup and sour cream. Yield: 2¹/₂ cups.

French Chicken Cordon Bleu

Rouladen in poultry form.

8 chicken breast filets
8 slices Danish ham
8 slices Swiss cheese
3 tablespoons chopped parsley
1/4 teaspoon pepper
2 eggs, beaten
1 cup Italian bread crumbs
1/4 cup margarine
1   10-ounce can cream of mushroom soup
1 cup sour cream

Rinse chicken and pat dry. Pound 1/4 inch thick with meat mallet. Top each filet with slice of ham and cheese; sprinkle with mixture of parsley and pepper. Roll to enclose filling; secure with wooden picks. Dip in eggs; roll in bread crumbs. Brown in margarine in heavy skillet. Place in 9x13-inch baking dish. Stir mixture of soup and sour cream into drippings in skillet. Pour over chicken. Bake at 350 degrees for 45 minutes. Serve with green vegetables and wild rice. Yield: 8 servings.

Indian Chicken Curry

2 tablespoons butter
2 tablespoons curry powder
1   28-ounce can tomatoes
2 tablespoons sugar
2 tablespoons chutney
1 envelope dry onion soup mix
2 chickens, cooked, boned
Cooked rice
Spanish peanuts, raisins, chutney and banana slices
Chopped eggs, tomato, onion and celery

Melt butter in skillet. Add curry powder. Stir in undrained tomatoes, sugar, chutney and soup mix. Cook for several minutes. Stir in chickens. Simmer for 15 minutes. Spoon over rice. Top with remaining ingredients. Yield: 8 servings.

Mexican Chicken Fajitas

1/2 cup fresh lime juice
1/3 cup vegetable oil
1/4 teaspoon crushed cumin seed
2 cloves of garlic, minced
1/4 teaspoon salt   1/8 teaspoon pepper
1 red hot pepper
2 chicken breasts, boned, cut into strips
1 onion, sliced into thin rings
11/2 green bell peppers, sliced into thin rings
1 cup shredded Cheddar cheese
Chopped tomato   Jalapeño pepper slices
Sliced black olives   Chopped green onions
Sour cream   Fresh Salsa
Guacamole (page 47)   Flour tortillas

Combine lime juice, oil, cumin, garlic, salt, pepper and hot pepper in bowl; mix well. Add chicken strips; stir well. Marinate for 30 minutes. Sauté chicken in skillet over high heat for 5 minutes or until light brown. Stir in onion and green pepper rings. Sauté for 2 minutes longer. Arrange chicken mixture, cheese, tomato, jalapeño pepper slices, olives, green onions, sour cream, Fresh Salsa, Guacamole and tortillas for buffet service. Fill tortillas with hot chicken and selected ingredients; roll up. Yield: 6 servings.

Fresh Salsa

3 tomatoes, chopped
3 fresh jalapeño peppers, chopped
3 tablespoons chopped onion
1 tablespoon chopped parsley
1/2 teaspoon salt   1 clove of garlic, crushed
11/2 tablespoons cider vinegar
1/4 teaspoon ground cumin   1/8 teaspoon sugar

Combine tomatoes, peppers, onion, parsley, salt, garlic, vinegar, cumin and sugar in bowl. Process a small amount at a time in food processor, pulsing at low speed. Pour into serving bowl. Yield: 3 cups.

Guacamole

2 avocados, finely chopped
1¹/₂ tablespoons lemon juice
1 tablespoon chopped fresh cilantro
2 cloves of garlic, crushed
1 teaspoon crushed dried basil   ¹/₂ teaspoon salt
1 tablespoon dried crushed red pepper
2 tablespoons salsa   2 teaspoons sliced green onions
1¹/₂ tablespoons slivered almonds, chopped

Process 1 avocado, lemon juice, cilantro, garlic, basil and salt in food processor at low speed. Spoon into serving bowl. Stir in remaining 1 avocado, red pepper, salsa, green onions and almonds. Yield: 2¹/₂ cups.

Italian Chicken Lasagna

4 cups sliced fresh mushrooms
2 cups chopped onions   ¹/₄ cup margarine
2 envelopes Hollandaise sauce mix
16 ounces lasagna noodles, cooked
2 pounds chicken, cooked, thinly sliced
Salt and pepper to taste   1 teaspoon basil
1 teaspoon oregano
3 cups shredded mozzarella cheese
1 cup Parmesan cheese
2   12-ounce cans asparagus tips, drained

Sauté mushrooms and onions in margarine in skillet. Prepare Hollandaise sauce using package directions. Spread a small amount in two 9x13-inch baking dishes. Layer half the noodles and half the chicken in prepared dishes. Sprinkle with salt and pepper. Add half the mushroom mixture and half the remaining Hollandaise sauce. Sprinkle with half the basil, oregano and half the cheeses. Add layers of all the asparagus, remaining noodles, chicken, salt, pepper, mushrooms, Hollandaise sauce, herbs and cheeses. Bake at 350 degrees for 35 minutes. Let stand for 10 minutes. Yield: 20 to 24 servings.

Italian Chicken Scampi

4 ounces chicken breast filets
2 tablespoons plus 2 teaspoons vegetable oil
3 tablespoons lemon juice
2 tablespoons Worcestershire sauce
1/4 cup unsweetened white grape juice
3 tablespoons Parmesan cheese   1 tablespoon parsley flakes
1 teaspoon oregano   1/8 teaspoon garlic powder
1/4 teaspoon salt   1/4 teaspoon pepper

Rinse chicken; cut into 1-inch strips. Combine with oil, lemon juice, Worcestershire sauce, juice, Parmesan cheese, parsley flakes, oregano, garlic powder, salt and pepper in bowl; mix well. Marinate in refrigerator for several hours to overnight. Drain, reserving marinade. Place chicken in shallow pan. Broil 8 inches from heat source until cooked through, turning once. Heat reserved marinade to serving temperature in saucepan. Pour over chicken in serving dish. Yield: 4 servings.

Russian Chicken Stroganoff

1/4 cup flour   1 teaspoon salt
1 teaspoon pepper   3 chicken breast filets
2 tablespoons butter   6 mushrooms
1 medium onion, chopped   4 teaspoons flour
4 teaspoons butter   1/2 teaspoon dry mustard
2 cups chicken broth
1 teaspoon tomato paste or catsup
1 cup sour cream   Cooked wide noodles

Mix 1/4 cup flour, salt and pepper in bowl. Rinse chicken and pat dry. Cut into strips. Coat well with flour mixture. Brown in 2 tablespoons butter in saucepan for 5 minutes. Add mushrooms and onion. Cook for 3 minutes. Remove chicken and vegetables with slotted spoon; set aside. Stir in 4 teaspoons flour, 4 teaspoons butter and dry mustard. Add chicken broth gradually. Cook for 3 minutes, stirring constantly. Stir in tomato paste and sour cream. Add chicken and vegetables. Heat just to serving temperature; do not boil. Spoon over noodles. Yield: 6 servings.

Indonesian Chicken Saté

6 boned skinned chicken breasts
1/2 cup melted butter or margarine
1/4 cup soy sauce   1 teaspoon crushed coriander
2 tablespoons fresh lime juice   1 small onion, thinly sliced
2 cloves of garlic, minced   1 tablespoon peanut oil
1 cup dry roasted peanuts   1/4 teaspoon minced gingerroot
1 or 2 small red chili peppers   1 tablespoon soy sauce
1 teaspoon sugar   2 tablespoons fresh lime juice
1/2 cup (about) boiling water

Rinse chicken and pat dry. Cut chicken into bite-sized pieces. Thread onto 12 bamboo skewers. Combine butter, 1/4 cup soy sauce, coriander and 2 tablespoons lime juice in small bowl; mix well. Brush over chicken. Grill chicken skewers 3 inches from hot coals for 15 minutes or until tender and brown, turning and basting frequently with butter mixture. Sauté onion and garlic in peanut oil in skillet until tender and golden. Combine with peanuts and remaining ingredients except boiling water in blender container. Process while adding enough boiling water gradually to make thick sauce for dipping. Garnish chicken skewers with kumquats; arrange on bed of yellow rice and serve with peanut sauce.
Yield: 4 to 6 servings.

French Poulet aux Pignons

1   3-pound chicken   1 lemon
4 to 6 tablespoons chopped herbs (thyme, marjoram, savory)
Olive oil   Salt and pepper   4 to 6 tablespoons pine nuts
1/3 cup white grape juice   Chopped fresh chervil

Rinse chicken and pat dry. Squeeze lemon inside chicken; place inside with 2 tablespoons of chopped herbs. Brush chicken with olive oil. Sprinkle with salt, pepper and remaining herbs. Place breast side down on rack in roasting pan. Roast at 400 degrees for 1 hour and 20 minutes. Turn and roast each side for 20 minutes, basting occasionally with pan drippings. Remove to platter. Add pine nuts to pan drippings. Cook over high heat until pine nuts are toasted, deglazing pan. Stir in grape juice. Pour sauce over chicken. Garnish with chervil. Yield: 4 to 6 servings.

Szechwan Chicken and Cashews

1 tablespoon soy sauce
1 tablespoon Chinese rice vinegar
4 chicken breast filets, cut into 3/4-inch cubes
1/4 cup vegetable oil
1/2 to 1 teaspoon crushed red pepper flakes
3 green onions, sliced diagonally
1 tablespoon minced fresh ginger
2 tablespoons soy sauce   1 tablespoon cornstarch
2 teaspoons sugar   1 teaspoon white vinegar
1/2 cup unsalted cashews   2 cups hot cooked rice

Combine 1 tablespoon soy sauce and rice vinegar in bowl; mix well. Pour over chicken in shallow dish. Marinate, covered, in refrigerator for 30 minutes. Drain, reserving marinade. Heat oil in wok or heavy skillet. Add red pepper to taste. Cook until black, stirring constantly. Add chicken. Stir-fry for 2 minutes. Remove chicken to dish. Add green onions and ginger to wok. Stir-fry for 1 minute. Add chicken. Cook for 2 minutes, stirring constantly. Combine remaining 2 tablespoons soy sauce, cornstarch, sugar and vinegar in bowl; mix well. Add with reserved marinade to chicken mixture. Cook until thickened, stirring constantly. Stir in cashews. Spoon over hot rice. Yield: 4 servings.

Tahitian Chicken

6 chicken thighs, skinned   1/4 cup flour
1 teaspoon paprika   1 teaspoon salt
1/8 teaspoon pepper   1/4 cup butter or margarine
3/4 cup orange juice   1/2 cup orange marmalade
3 tablespoons cornstarch   1/2 cup cold water
1/4 cup slivered almonds

Rinse chicken and pat dry. Coat with mixture of flour, paprika, salt and pepper. Brown in butter in skillet; remove to 8x8-inch baking dish. Heat orange juice and marmalade in saucepan until marmalade melts. Stir in mixture of cornstarch and water. Cook until thickened, stirring constantly. Pour sauce over chicken; sprinkle with almonds. Bake at 350 degrees for 50 minutes. Yield: 6 servings.

What a great invention—whoever first married honey and mustard was a genius! Then came the curry powder and a truly indescribable treat awaits. Serve the chicken with rice for an oriental flair, with black beans for a hint of the Caribbean, or with French fries and a dipping sauce of equal parts mustard and honey for just plain enjoyment.

Honey and Curry Chicken

(English Version)

1/3 cup margarine
1/4 cup Dijon mustard
1/3 cup honey
2 1/2 teaspoons curry powder
1/4 teaspoon cayenne pepper
3 whole chicken breasts, boned, skinned, split

Melt margarine in small saucepan. Add mustard, honey, curry powder and cayenne pepper; mix well. Bring to a boil, stirring constantly. Rinse chicken; pat dry. Arrange chicken in greased 9-inch square baking pan. Pour mustard mixture over chicken. Bake, covered, at 375 degrees for 20 minutes. Baste with pan juices. Bake, uncovered, for 20 minutes. Yield: 2 to 3 servings.

Poulet au Curry et Miel

(French Translation)

¹/₂ tasse de margarine
¹/₄ tasse de moutard de Dijon
¹/₃ tasse de miel
2¹/₂ cuillerées à café de curry en poudre
¹/₂ cuillerée à café de poivre de Cayenne
6 escalopes de poulet

Faites fondre la margarine dans une petite casserole. Incorporez le moutard, le miel, le curry et le poivre de Cayenne; remuez bien. Portez à l'ébullition en remuant constamment. Rincez les escalopes de poulet et séchez-les. Mettez-les dans un plat allant au four préalableement graissé. Nappez-les avec la sauce moutard. Couvrez le plat avec du papier alu et mettez-le au four. Faites cuire à 375 degrés F. pendant 20 minutes. Arrosez les escalopes avec le jus du cuisson. Remettez le plat au four pendant 20 minutes de plus. Pour 6 personnes.

Honig und Curry Hähnchen

(German Translation)

¹/₃ Tasse Margarine
¹/₄ Tasse Dijon Senf
¹/₃ Tasse Honig
2¹/₂ Teelöffel Currypulver
¹/₄ Teelöffel Cayennepfeffer
6 Hähnchenbrüste, ohne Knochen, enthäutet

Margarine in einem kleinen Saucentopf schmelzen. Die nächsten 4 Zutaten hinzufügen; gut mischen. Unter ständigem Rühren zum Kochen bringen. Das Hähnchen abwaschen; trockentupfen. Die Hähnchenteile in eine eingefettete etwa 25x25 cm große Bratform geben. Die Senfmischung über das Hähnchen gießen. Bei 375 Grad Fahrenheit zugedeckt 20 Minuten lang backen lassen. Mit dem Bratfond übergießen. Aufgedeckt weitere 20 Minuten backen. Für 6 Personen.

Pollo al miele e curry

(Italian Translation)

$1/3$ **tazza margarina**
$1/4$ **tazza senape di Dijon**
$1/3$ **tazza miele**
$2 1/2$ **cucchiaini curry in polvere**
$1/4$ **cucchiaino pepe cayenne**
6 petti di pollo, disossati e scuoiati

Sciogliere la margarina in una piccola pentola. Aggiungere i prossimi 4 ingredienti; mescolare bene. Far bollire, girandolo costantemente. Risciacquare e asciugare il pollo. Mettere il pollo in una casseruola di 9 pollici quadri. Versare la salsa sul pollo. Cuocere al forno, con coperchio, 20 minuti. Ungere con il sugo nella casseruola. Cuocere ancora 20 minuti senza coperchio. Porzioni: 6.

Pollo con miel y curry

(Spanish Translation)

$1/3$ **taza de margarina**
$1/4$ **taza de mostaza dijon**
$1/3$ **taza de miel**
$2 1/2$ **cucharaditas de polvo de curry**
$1/4$ **cucharadita de pimienta sacada del chile**
6 pechugas de gallina, sin hueso y sin piel

Derretir la margarina en una olla pequeña. Agregar la mostaza, la miel, el curry y la pimienta; mezclar bien. Hacer hervir la mezcla, dándole vuelta continuamente. Enjuagar el pollo; secarlo. Meter el pollo en una cacerola engrasada; que mida la cacerola 9 por 9 pulgadas. Echar al pollo la mezcla con mostaza. Cocinar al horno, tapada la cacerola, a 375 grados, por 20 minutos. Rociar con el jugo que quede en la cacerola. Cocinar, destapada la cacerola, por 20 minutos. Rendimiento: 6 porciones.

Cornish Hens Vera Cruz

(Mexican)

6 slices bacon   2 cups rice
1/4 cup minced onion   1 8-ounce can tomatoes
1 1/2 cups water   Salt and pepper to taste
1 teaspoon cumin   2 teaspoons garlic powder
1 teaspoon cayenne pepper
1/2 cup shredded Cheddar cheese
1/2 cup lime juice   1/2 cup oil
6 Cornish game hens, thawed, rinsed, patted dry

Cook bacon in large skillet until crisp. Remove to paper towel to drain; crumble. Sauté rice and onion in drippings in skillet over medium heat until rice is light brown. Stir in tomatoes and 1 1/2 cups water. Add bacon, salt, pepper, cumin, garlic powder, cayenne pepper and cheese; mix well. Add additional water if rice appears crunchy and dry. Simmer, covered, until water is absorbed and rice is tender. Combine lime juice and oil in small bowl. Coat hens with lime juice mixture. Stuff hens with rice mixture. Place in greased roasting pan. Roast at 375 degrees for 30 to 45 minutes or until tender. Yield: 6 servings.

Greek Turkey Pitas

1 pound turkey breakfast sausage
2 tablespoons lemon juice   Pinch of cinnamon
Pinch of nutmeg   1 clove of garlic, minced
2 tablespoons chopped mint
1/2 teaspoon oregano   1 tablespoon chopped parsley
1 onion, thinly sliced   1 tomato, chopped
1/2 cup sliced deli-style pickles
6 small pita rounds, cut into halves
8 ounces plain yogurt

Shape turkey sausage into tiny balls. Brown in large skillet sprayed with nonstick cooking spray; drain. Add lemon juice, seasonings, onion, tomato and pickle slices. Simmer, covered, for 2 to 3 minutes or just until vegetables are tender-crisp. Spoon mixture into pita pockets; top with yogurt. Yield: 4 to 6 servings.

Bouillabaisse

*Classic **French** catch-of-the-day seafood stew.*

1/2 cup chopped onion   1/2 cup chopped celery
1 clove of garlic, minced
1/4 cup butter or margarine
1 pound fresh fish filets, skinned, cubed
1 bay leaf, crushed   1/4 teaspoon thyme
Salt and black pepper to taste
Red pepper to taste   1 20-ounce can tomatoes
1 cup fish stock or water
1/2 pint fresh oysters, shelled
1/2 pound shrimp, peeled

Sauté onion, celery and garlic in butter in 6-quart saucepan until tender. Add cubed fish, bay leaf, thyme, salt, black pepper, red pepper, tomatoes and fish stock; mix well. Simmer for 10 minutes. Add oysters and shrimp. Simmer for 10 minutes longer. Serve with French bread. Yield: 6 to 8 servings.

Linguine with Clam Sauce

(Italian)

1 10-ounce can clams   2 tablespoons minced onion
2 tablespoons minced celery
3 tablespoons margarine
3/4 cup sliced mushrooms
2 tablespoons flour   1 cup milk
1 tablespoon chopped parsley
Salt and pepper to taste
1 16-ounce package linguine, cooked

Drain clams, reserving liquid; chop clams. Sauté onion and celery in margarine in small saucepan. Add mushrooms. Cook for 2 to 3 minutes or until tender. Stir in flour. Add reserved clam liquid and milk. Cook until thickened, stirring constantly. Add clams, parsley, salt and pepper. Cook until heated through. Spoon over linguine. Serve with tossed salad and dinner rolls. Yield: 8 servings.

Greek Seafood Baklava

8 ounces shrimp, peeled, deveined
8 ounces scallops   8 ounces fish
1   10-ounce package frozen chopped spinach, thawed
2 carrots, thinly sliced   1 medium onion, chopped
1/2 teaspoon sage   1/4 teaspoon salt
1 cup dry bread crumbs
6 sheets frozen phyllo dough, thawed

Cut shrimp, scallops and fish into 1-inch pieces. Squeeze spinach to remove excess moisture. Sauté carrots and onion in skillet sprayed with butter-flavored nonstick cooking spray. Add spinach, seafood, sage and salt. Cook until seafood is opaque. Stir in 1/4 cup bread crumbs; remove from heat. Place 1 sheet of phyllo dough on waxed paper. Spray with nonstick cooking spray. Sprinkle with about 2 tablespoons bread crumbs. Repeat process with remaining sheets of dough and bread crumbs. Spread seafood mixture lengthwise down 1 side of dough, covering 1/4 of dough. Roll dough from seafood side to enclose filling. Tuck ends under; place on baking sheet sprayed with nonstick cooking spray. Bake at 400 degrees for 20 minutes. Let stand for 5 minutes. Slice to serve. Yield: 6 servings.

Far Eastern Seafood Stir-Fry

2 tablespoons peanut oil
1/3 pound bay scallops   1/3 pound shrimp
1/3 pound crab meat, cut into bite-sized pieces
1 large onion, cut into 1/4-inch rings
2 large green bell peppers, cut into 1/4-inch slices
2 cups mushrooms, cut into quarters
Cooked rice   Soy sauce to taste

Heat peanut oil in wok. Add scallops, shrimp and crab meat. Stir-fry for 2 minutes or until opaque. Remove with slotted spoon to bowl. Add onion, green peppers and mushrooms to wok. Stir-fry until tender-crisp. Add crab meat mixture. Stir-fry for 1 minute longer or until heated through. Spoon over hot cooked rice. Drizzle with soy sauce. Yield: 4 servings.

Thai Coconut Shrimp

1 pound medium shrimp
1 cup unsweetened coconut milk
1/2 teaspoon Chinese chili sauce
1/4 teaspoon salt   1 tablespoon peanut oil
1 tablespoon unsalted butter
4 cloves of garlic, finely minced
4 ounces small mushrooms
1/4 cup chopped green onions
1/4 cup chopped fresh mint leaves
1/4 cup chopped fresh basil   1 tablespoon cornstarch
1 tablespoon water   1 tablespoon lime juice

Peel, devein and butterfly shrimp; pat dry. Chill in refrigerator. Combine coconut milk, chili sauce and salt in bowl; mix well. Set aside. Heat peanut oil and butter in wok or sauté pan over high heat until bubbly. Add garlic. Stir-fry for several seconds. Add shrimp. Stir-fry for 2 minutes or until opaque. Add mushrooms, green onions, mint and basil. Stir-fry for 15 seconds. Stir in coconut milk mixture. Bring to a boil. Stir in mixture of cornstarch and water. Cook until thickened, stirring constantly. Stir in lime juice. Spoon onto heated platter. Garnish with basil leaves and/or mint leaves. Serve with steamed white or brown rice. Yield: 4 servings.

Mexican Chilies Rellenos

4 egg yolks   4 egg whites
1/4 cup flour   3/4 teaspoon baking powder
1/4 teaspoon salt   1 small onion, chopped
2 cups shredded sharp Cheddar cheese
6 canned green chilies
3 tablespoons oil

Beat egg yolks in mixer bowl until thick and lemon-colored. Beat egg whites in mixer bowl until stiff peaks form. Fold in egg yolks. Sift in flour, baking powder and salt; mix well. Combine onion and cheese in bowl; mix well. Stuff carefully into chilies. Dip chilies into batter, coating well. Fry in oil in skillet until brown on both sides, turning once. May substitute seeded fresh chilies or frozen chilies for canned chilies. Yield: 6 servings.

Chilies Rellenos Casserole

*Be sure to remove the seeds from the chilies if your taste buds can't enjoy the hot and spicy flavor of this **Mexican** dish.*

2 7-ounce cans whole green chilies
8 ounces Cheddar cheese, shredded
8 ounces Monterey Jack cheese, shredded
3 eggs
3 tablespoons flour
1 12-ounce can evaporated milk
7 ounces green chili salsa

Layer half the chilies, Cheddar cheese, remaining chilies and Monterey Jack cheese in greased 8x12-inch baking dish. Beat eggs, flour and evaporated milk in mixer bowl. Pour over layers. Bake at 325 degrees for 40 minutes. Top with salsa. Bake for 5 minutes longer or until bubbly. Yield: 6 servings.

New Mexico-Style Enchiladas

The flat stacked enchiladas with eggs are the New Mexico-style but this yummy sauce is strictly for Gringos.

1 medium onion, chopped
1 tablespoon shortening
1 cup drained canned tomatoes
1 cup chopped green chilies
1/2 cup whipping cream
6 corn tortillas
Shortening for frying tortillas
1 cup shredded Cheddar cheese
Fried eggs

Sauté onion in 1 tablespoon shortening in skillet. Add tomatoes and green chilies; mix well. Stir in cream gradually. Simmer for 5 minutes. Fry tortillas in hot shortening in heavy skillet until crisp. Alternate layers of tortillas, sauce and cheese on serving plates. Bake at 350 degrees for 5 to 10 minutes or until cheese melts. Top with fried eggs. Garnish with shredded lettuce. Yield: 2 servings.

Cantonese-Style Egg Foo Yong

A Chinese omelet.

5 large eggs
1/2 cup shredded cooked meat, poultry or fish
1/2 cup slivered celery stalks
1/2 cup slivered mushrooms
1 cup bean sprouts or slivered bamboo shoots
1/4 cup slivered onion
1 teaspoon salt
1/4 teaspoon MSG (optional)
Pepper to taste
Vegetable oil for frying
Sauce

Mix eggs, meat, celery stalks, mushrooms, bamboo shoots, onion, salt, MSG and pepper in large bowl; do not beat. Heat 1/2 cup oil in deep skillet, Dutch oven or wok over medium heat. Spoon 1/4 of the egg mixture into oil carefully. Cook until edges are brown; turn gently. Brown on other side. Remove to plate. Fry remaining 3 portions in same manner, adding additonal oil if needed. Serve hot, plain or with Sauce. Yield: 2 to 3 servings.

Sauce

2 1/2 tablespoons flour
1/4 cup cold water
1   13 3/4-ounce can ready-to-serve chicken broth
1 teaspoon catsup
1 tablespoon soy sauce
1/2 teaspoon salt

Combine flour and water in saucepan; blend well. Stir in broth, catsup, soy sauce and salt. Cook until thickened, stirring constantly. Yield: 2 cups.

Artichoke Frittata

*Cut these baked **Italian** eggs into small squares to
serve as appetizers, too.*

**1   12-ounce jar marinated artichoke hearts
4 eggs, beaten
8 ounces small curd cottage cheese
1 small onion, chopped
1/8 teaspoon rosemary   1/8 teaspoon thyme
1/8 teaspoon basil
1/8 teaspoon marjoram**

Drain artichokes, reserving 2 tablespoons marinade. Combine
artichokes, reserved marinade, eggs, cottage cheese, onion,
rosemary, thyme, basil and marjoram in bowl; mix well. Pour into
greased 8-inch square baking dish. Bake at 350 degrees for 30
minutes or until light brown and set. Cut into squares.
Yield: 4 servings.

Basic French Omelet

*Delicious plain or filled with meat, cheese or vegetables for
breakfast or dinner. Surprising with fruit for brunch or dessert.*

**3 eggs, at room temperature
1 tablespoon water
1 1/2 teaspoons peanut oil   1 1/2 teaspoons butter
Salt and pepper to taste**

Preheat omelet pan on medium heat. Whip eggs with a table
fork in small bowl. Add water; whip again. Place oil and butter
in preheated pan at the same time. Heat until butter stops foaming.
Whip eggs several times; pour into pan. Lift edge with wooden
spatula to allow wet portion of mixture to run under the omelet.
Add salt and pepper. Slide omelet onto plate. Fold omelet over in
half. Garnish with parsley or filling. Serve hot. Yield: 1 serving.

Pasta is such a short simple word for a product that is so many things to so many people—simple or elaborate in shape—there are dozens of them; good in rich creamy dishes or light salads; energy packed for athletes or tummy filling for dieters. Italians may think they invented pasta but Marco Polo would tell a different story.

Ham and Cheese Fettucini

(English Version)

1/2 cup butter
1/2 cup whipping cream
3/4 cup grated Parmesan cheese
2 tablespoons chopped parsley
8 ounces fettucini, cooked, drained
1 cup chopped cooked ham

Combine butter and whipping cream in small saucepan. Cook over low heat until butter melts. Stir in cheese and parsley. Pour over hot pasta in large bowl; toss to mix well. Add ham; toss gently. Yield: 8 servings.

Fettucine au Jambon et Fromage

(French Translation)

1/2 tasse de beurre
1/2 tasse de crème épaisse
3/4 tasse de fromage de Parmesan, râpé
2 cuillerées à soupe de persil haché
8 onces de fettucine, cuits et égouttés
1 tasse de jambon cuit, coupé en dés

Mettez le beurre et la crème dans une petite casserole. Faites chauffer au feu doux pour fondre le beurre. Ajoutez le fromage et le persil. Versez la sauce sur les fettucine dans un grand saladier et mélangez bien. Ajoutez le jambon en remuant doucement. Pour 8 personnes.

Schinken und Käse Fettucine

(German Translation)

1/2 Tasse Butter
1/2 Tasse süße Sahne
3/4 Tasse geriebenen Parmesankäse
2 Eßlöffel gehackte Petersilie
8 Unzen Fettucine, gekocht, abgetropft
1 Tasse kleingeschnittenen gekochten Schinken

Butter und süße Sahne zusammen in einen kleinen Saucentopf geben. Auf kleiner Flamme so lange kochen, bis die Butter geschmolzen ist. Käse und Petersilie dazufügen. Über die heißen Nudeln in einer großen Schüssel gießen; gut mischen. Schinken hinzufügen; sanft umrühren. Für 8 Personen.

Fettuccine al prosciutto e formaggio

(Italian Translation)

¹/₂ tazza burro
¹/₂ tazza panna
³/₄ tazza parmigiano grattato
2 cucchiai prezzemolo tritato
8 once fettuccine, cotte e scolate
1 tazza prosciutto cotto, tritato

Mescolare insieme il burro e la panna in un piccolo tegame. Cuocere a fuoco lento finché il burro sia sciolto. Aggiungere il formaggio e il prezzemolo. Versare sulla pasta calda in una zuppiera; mescolare bene. Aggiungere il prosciutto e mescolare lievemente. Porzioni: 8.

Fideos fettuccini con jamón y queso

(Spanish Translation)

¹/₂ taza de mantequilla
¹/₂ taza de nata no batida
³/₄ taza de queso parmesano rallado
2 cucharadas de perejil picado
8 onzas de fideos fettuccini, hervidos, quitada el agua
1 taza de jamón cocido y picado

Combinar la mantequilla y la nata en una olla pequeña. Calentar a fuego lento hasta derretirse la mantequilla. Agregar el queso y el perejil, y mezclarse. Echar a los fideos, y mezclar bien. Agregar el jamón, mezclar bien, pero suave. Rendimiento: 8 porciones.

Fettucini Alfredo Florentine

(Italian)

1   16-ounce package fettucini   1 onion, chopped
1 pound mushrooms, sliced   ¹/₂ cup butter or margarine
1   10-ounce package frozen chopped spinach, thawed
Garlic salt to taste   Pepper to taste   16 ounces sour cream
1 cup shredded Romano cheese   ¹/₄ cup milk

Cook fettucini *al dente* using package directions. Sauté onion and mushrooms in butter in skillet until tender. Stir in spinach, garlic salt and pepper. Add sour cream to spinach mixture; mix well. Cook over low heat until heated through; do not boil. Remove from heat. Stir in cheese until melted. Add milk if necessary for desired consistency. Place fettucini on serving plate; top with spinach mixture. Yield: 8 servings.

Tortellini with Tomato Pesto

(Italian)

¹/₂ stick pepperoni, cut into small pieces
3 tablespoons Dijon mustard   4 cloves of garlic, minced
1 tablespoon fennel seed
1   7-ounce jar sun-dried tomatoes, drained
1¹/₂ cups olive oil   2 tablespoons lemon juice
Salt and pepper to taste
2 pounds meat or cheese tortellini, cooked, drained
2 ripe tomatoes, seeded, chopped
1 yellow bell pepper, chopped
1 stick pepperoni, thinly sliced   Lettuce leaves
¹/₂ cup chopped fresh parsley
3 tablespoons chopped fresh basil   Black olives

Combine pepperoni pieces, mustard, garlic, fennel seed and sun-dried tomatoes in blender container. Add oil in fine stream, processing constantly at high speed until mixture is smooth. Mix in lemon juice, salt and pepper. Combine cooked tortellini, tomatoes, yellow pepper and sliced pepperoni in large bowl. Add sauce; toss well. Serve in large lettuce-lined salad bowl. Sprinkle with parsley, basil and black olives. Yield: 8 servings.

Desserts

Black Forest Chocolate Cheesecake

1¼ cups graham cracker crumbs
¼ cup Hershey's baking cocoa   ¼ cup sugar
½ cup melted butter   16 ounces cream cheese, softened
1 cup sour cream   1¼ cups sugar
½ cup Hershey's baking cocoa   3 eggs
2 teaspoons almond extract   1 cup whipping cream
¼ cup confectioners' sugar   ½ teaspoon almond extract
1 21-ounce can cherry pie filling, chilled

Combine first 4 ingredients in bowl; mix well. Press over bottom of 9-inch springform pan. Combine cream cheese, sour cream and 1¼ cups sugar in mixer bowl; beat until smooth. Add ½ cup cocoa, eggs and 2 teaspoons almond extract; beat just until blended. Pour into prepared pan. Bake at 350 degrees for 45 to 50 minutes or until center is almost set. Cool on wire rack for 30 minutes. Loosen from side of pan; remove side. Chill, covered, until serving time. Beat whipping cream with ¼ cup confectioners' sugar and ½ teaspoon almond extract in mixer bowl. Pipe around edge of cheesecake; spoon pie filling into center. Yield: 12 servings.

German Choco-Cherry Cupcakes

1½ cups flour   1 cup sugar
¼ cup Hershey's baking cocoa   1 teaspoon baking soda
½ teaspoon salt   1 cup water   ⅔ cup vegetable oil
1 tablespoon white vinegar   1 teaspoon vanilla extract
¼ cup milk   2 tablespoons flour   ¼ cup shortening
1 teaspoon almond extract   2¼ cups confectioners' sugar
¼ cup maraschino cherries, drained

Combine first 5 ingredients in mixer bowl. Add water, oil, vinegar and vanilla; mix well. Spoon into paper-lined muffin cups. Bake at 350 degrees for 15 to 20 minutes or until cupcakes test done. Cool. Blend milk and 2 tablespoons flour in small saucepan. Bring to a boil over low heat, stirring constantly with wire whisk. Refrigerate until chilled. Combine milk mixture and remaining ingredients except cherries in mixer bowl; beat until smooth. Stir in cherries. May tint with red food coloring if desired. Yield: 1½ dozen.

Photograph for these recipes is on previous page.

Italian Anise Cookies

*Anise is a popular flavor in European cooking
that closely resembles licorice.*

6 eggs
1 cup oil
1 cup sugar
1 teaspoon vanilla extract
2 tablespoons baking powder
4 cups flour
4 to 6 teaspoons aniseed
3/4 cup chopped walnuts

Beat eggs in large mixer bowl. Add oil, sugar and vanilla; mix well. Stir in baking powder and flour until moistened. Stir in aniseed and walnuts. Shape dough into 4 loaves on cookie sheet. Bake at 350 degrees for 30 minutes. Cut into slices while hot. Arrange on cookie sheet. Toast under broiler until light brown. Cool on wire rack. Yield: 4 dozen.

Berlinerkranze

*These **German** cookies resemble pretzels in shape but
taste more like shortbread.*

1 cup melted butter
1/2 cup sugar
2 egg yolks
2 hard-boiled egg yolks, mashed
2 cups flour
1 teaspoon vanilla extract
1 egg white, slightly beaten
Crushed loaf sugar or coarse sugar

Combine butter, 1/2 cup sugar, egg yolks, flour and vanilla in bowl; mix well. Chill for 1 hour. Shape into pencil-sized pieces. Bend each into single knot. Dip into egg white; coat with crushed sugar. Place on large ungreased cookie sheet. Bake at 400 degrees for 10 minutes or until golden brown. Cool on wire rack. Yield: 6 dozen.

Mexican Biscochitos

Substitute the traditional wine with orange or pineapple juice.

1 cup lard   1/2 cup sugar
1 egg
3 cups flour
1 1/2 teaspoons baking powder
1/2 teaspoon salt
3 tablespoons sweet wine
1 teaspoon aniseed
1/4 cup sugar
1 tablespoon cinnamon

Cream lard and 1/2 cup sugar in mixer bowl until light. Beat in egg until fluffy. Sift flour, baking powder and salt together. Add to creamed mixture. Stir in wine and aniseed. Roll dough 1/4 inch thick on floured surface. Cut into squares. Sprinkle mixture of 1/4 cup sugar and cinnamon on top. Place on cookie sheet. Bake at 350 degrees for 15 to 20 minutes or until golden brown. Remove to wire rack to cool. May substitute shortening for lard. Yield: 4 dozen.

Italian Biscotti

Made for dunking.

6 eggs, beaten
1 cup sugar
1 teaspoon salt
1 tablespoon anise extract
3 cups flour
1 tablespoon baking powder
8 ounces sliced almonds

Combine eggs, sugar, salt and anise extract in bowl; mix well. Add flour and baking powder gradually; mix well. Stir in almonds. Divide into 3 portions. Shape into balls. Let stand in warm place for 15 minutes. Shape into 2-inch long ropes. Place 2 inches apart on cookie sheet. Let stand for 10 to 15 minutes. Bake at 350 degrees for 25 to 30 minutes or until light brown. Cut into slices. Place on cookie sheet. Toast in oven. Yield: 3 dozen.

Filled Italian Cookies

2 cups chopped dates   1/2 cup butter
2 cups chopped pecans   1 cup raisins
1/2 cup grated orange rind   1/2 cup sugar
2 tablespoons rum flavoring
5 eggs, slightly beaten   2/3 cup vegetable oil
1 cup sugar   2 tablespoons baking powder
1/2 teaspoon vanilla extract   4 cups flour
1 cup confectioners' sugar

Combine dates, butter, pecans, raisins, orange rind, 1/2 cup sugar and rum flavoring in saucepan. Bring to a boil; reduce heat. Cook until thickened, stirring constantly. Let stand until cool. Combine eggs, oil, 1 cup sugar, baking powder and vanilla in mixer bowl; mix well. Add flour; mix well. Divide dough into 6 portions. Roll each portion into 5-inch wide rectangle on lightly floured surface. Spread each rectangle with filling. Roll from long side to enclose filling. Place seam side down 2 inches apart on ungreased cookie sheet. Bake at 375 degrees for 15 minutes. Remove to wire racks to cool. Roll in confectioners' sugar. Slice rolls diagonally. May substitute pecans for dates or water for rum flavoring if desired. Yield: 6 dozen.

Dutch Jan Hagel

1 cup butter, softened   1/2 cup sugar
1/2 cup packed brown sugar
1 egg yolk   2 cups flour
1/4 teaspoon salt
1/2 teaspoon cinnamon   1 egg white
1 tablespoon water
1/2 cup chopped almonds

Cream butter, sugar and brown sugar in mixer bowl until light and fluffy. Stir in egg yolk. Add mixture of flour, salt and cinnamon; mix well. Press into ungreased 10x15-inch baking pan. Beat egg white with water. Brush over dough. Sprinkle almonds over top. Bake at 325 degrees for 15 minutes or until golden brown. Cut into diamond shapes while warm. Cool. Yield: 3 dozen.

German Lebkuchen

3/4 cup packed brown sugar
1 egg   1 cup honey, warmed
1 tablespoon lemon juice
3 cups sifted flour   1/2 teaspoon baking soda
1/2 teaspoon salt   1 teaspoon nutmeg   1 teaspoon allspice
1 1/4 teaspoons cinnamon   1 1/4 teaspoons cloves
1 1/2 teaspoons grated lemon rind
1/3 cup finely chopped citron
1/3 cup finely chopped nuts   2 cups confectioners' sugar
3 tablespoons water

Beat brown sugar and egg in mixer bowl until light and fluffy. Beat in honey and lemon juice. Sift flour, baking soda, salt and spices together. Add lemon rind and 1 cup dry mixture to honey mixture; beat until smooth. Stir in remaining dry mixture. Add citron and nuts; mix well. Chill, covered, overnight. Roll dough 1/2 at a time to 1/4-inch thickness on lightly floured surface; cut with 2-inch round cookie cutter. Place 2 inches apart on lightly greased cookie sheet. Bake at 375 degrees for 15 minutes. Remove to wire rack. Cool slightly. Blend confectioners' sugar with water in bowl. Brush over warm cookies. Cool completely. Store in airtight container in cool dry place for 2 to 3 weeks before serving.
Yield: 3 dozen.

French Almond Madeleines

6 tablespoons unsalted butter, softened
2 tablespoons toasted almond oil
2 egg yolks   2/3 cup sugar   1 cup sifted flour
1 teaspoon baking powder   2 egg whites, stiffly beaten
1/4 cup ground toasted almonds

Cream butter and almond oil in bowl. Beat egg yolks and sugar in mixer bowl. Add creamed mixture and mixture of flour and baking powder. Fold in egg whites and ground almonds. Fill 24 buttered and floured madeleine molds 1/2 full. Bake at 400 degrees for 10 to 15 minutes or until golden brown. Cool on wire rack.
Yield: 2 dozen.

Cookies can be any size or shape imaginable. They can be tiny, dainty, lightly flavored and exactly right for teas and delicate nibbles or huge, hearty, tummy filling and a child's delight. These cookies, in many languages, are the best of all worlds—appealing to both imagination and taste buds.

Cat's Tongues

(English Version)

¹/₃ cup flour
Pinch of salt
¹/₄ cup butter, softened
¹/₃ cup sugar
3 egg whites
¹/₂ teaspoon vanilla extract

Sift flour and salt together. Cream butter and sugar in small mixer bowl until light and fluffy. Beat egg whites in small bowl until stiff peaks form. Add flour mixture, vanilla and egg whites alternately to creamed mixture, mixing well after each addition. Spoon into pastry bag fitted with ¹/₄-inch plain tube. Pipe 3-inch long pencils of batter onto 2 greased and floured cookie sheets, leaving space for cookies to spread. Bake at 450 degrees for 6 to 8 minutes or until edges are golden brown. Remove to wire rack to cool. Yield: 3 dozen.

Langues de Chat

(French Translation)

1/3 **tasse de farine   Une pincée de sel**
1/4 **tasse de beurre ramolli**
1/3 **tasse de sucre semoule**
3 blancs d'œuf
1/2 **cuillerée à café d'extrait de vanille**

Tamisez la farine et le sel dans un grand saladier. Battez le beurre avec un mixer électrique. Faites monter les blancs d'œuf en neige. Ajoutez la farine, la vanille et les blancs d'œufs en neige tour à tour au beurre, en remuant après chaque addition. Mettez la pâte dans une poche à douille. Tracez des lignes de pâte de 3 pouces de longueur sur 2 tôles beurrées et farinées, en laissant de l'espace entre chaque biscuit. Mettez-les au four et faites cuire à 450 degrés pendant 6 à 8 minutes ou jusqu'à légèrement dorés. Retirez-les et faites-les refroidir sur une grille. Pour 40 biscuits.

Katzenzungen

(German Translation)

1/3 **Tasse Mehl   Eine Prise Salz**
1/4 **Tasse erweichte Butter**
1/3 **Tasse Zucker**
3 Eiweiß
1/2 **Teelöffel Vanilleextrakt**

Mehl und Salz in eine große Schüssel sieben. Butter in Mixschüssel cremig rühren. Zucker hinzufügen, Masse schlagen, bis sie locker und flockig ist. Eiweiß in einer Schüssel zu festen Eischnee schlagen. Mehl, Vanille und Eiweiß abwechselnd zur Buttermischung hinzufügen, wobei nach jedem Hinzufügen gut zu mischen ist. In Spritzbeutel mit 1/2cm runden Tülle löffeln. Ca. 7-8cm große Strahlenbündel aus Teig auf 2 eingefettete und bemehlte Backbleche spritzen, dabei Platz lassen, damit die Plätzchen noch gehen können. Bei 450 Grad Fahrenheit 6 bis 8 Minuten bis die Enden goldbraun sind backen. Zum Abkühlen auf Gitter geben. Ergibt 40 Plätzchen.

Lingue di gatto

(Italian Translation)

¹/₃ tazza farina   Pizzico di sale
¹/₄ tazza burro, ammorbidito
¹/₃ tazza zucchero   3 bianchi di uovo
¹/₂ cucchiaino vaniglia

Passare la farina e il sale per uno spargifarina in una scodella grande. Sbattere il burro in scodella. Aggiungere lo zucchero, sbattendo finché leggero. Montare i bianchi di uovo in una piccola scodella. Aggiungere la farina, la vaniglia e i bianchi di uovo alternativamente, mescolando bene. Mettere in un sacco da pasta con il tubo da ¹/₄ pollice. Spremere in "matite" da 3 pollici su due teglie imburrate e infarinate, lasciando spazio abbastanza perché estendano. Cuocere a 450 gradi 6 a 8 minuti finché dorate. Rinfrescare su una rastrelliera. Porzioni: 40.

Galletas (lenguas de gato)

(Spanish Translation)

¹/₃ taza de harina   una pizca de sal
¹/₄ taza de mantequilla ablandada
¹/₃ taza de azúcar   3 claras de huevo
¹/₂ cucharadita de concentrado de vainilla

Cernerse la harina y la sal en una fuente grande. En otra fuente, formar nata de la mantequilla. Agregarse el azúcar a la mantequilla, formando una mezcla liviana y esponjada. Batir las claras de huevo en una fuente pequeña, hasta formarse pequeños picos. Agregarse a la nata de mantequilla, uno por uno, la harina, el concentrado de vainilla y las claras de huevo, revolviendo bien la mezcla después de agregarle cada ingrediente. Echar esta mezcla en una bolsa para pasteles al que se le coloca un tubo regular de ¹/₄ pulgada. En dos chapas engrasadas con mantequilla, y rociadas de harina, formar lápices de 3 pulgadas de largura, dejándoles espacio a las galletas, que van a hincharse. Cocinar al horno a 450 grados por 6 u 8 minutos, hasta dorarse los márgenes. Sacar las galletas y meterlas en una rejilla hasta enfriarse. Rendimiento: 40 galletas.

French Marzipan Cookies

Notice that these almost candy-like cookies have no flour.
The ground almonds serve a similar purpose.

1/2 cup sugar
3/4 cup ground almonds
Grated rind of 1 orange
2 egg yolks
1/8 teaspoon almond extract
1/4 cup confectioners' sugar
1/4 cup sliced almonds

Mix sugar, ground almonds and orange rind in bowl. Add egg yolks and almond extract; mix well. Chill for several minutes. Roll 1/8 inch thick on surface sprinkled with confectioners' sugar. Cut with 2-inch cookie cutter. Press several sliced almonds into each cookie. Place on greased cookie sheet. Bake at 375 degrees for 8 minutes or until golden brown. Cool on wire rack.
Yield: 1 1/2 dozen.

Mexican Wedding Cookies

Greek Kourabiades are another version. Be sure to roll cooled
cookies in more confectioners' sugar before serving.

1 cup confectioners' sugar
1/2 cup butter, softened
1 teaspoon vanilla extract
1 cup flour
1 cup finely chopped pecans

Combine confectioners' sugar, butter, vanilla, flour and pecans in bowl; mix well. Shape into balls. Place on ungreased cookie sheet. Bake at 375 degrees for 25 minutes or until light brown. Roll hot cookies in additional confectioners' sugar. Yield: 2 dozen.

Moravian Cookies

¹/₂ cup butter   1 cup molasses
¹/₃ cup packed brown sugar
³/₄ teaspoon ginger
³/₄ teaspoon cloves   ³/₄ teaspoon cinnamon
¹/₄ teaspoon nutmeg
¹/₄ teaspoon allspice
Dash of salt   ³/₄ teaspoon baking soda
3³/₄ cups sifted flour

Combine butter and molasses in saucepan. Heat until butter is melted; remove from heat. Stir in next 8 ingredients. Add flour gradually; mix well. Chill, tightly wrapped in plastic wrap, for 1 week. Roll thinly on lightly floured surface. Cut with cookie cutter. Place on greased cookie sheet. Punch hole for hangers if desired. Bake at 350 degrees until golden brown. Cool on wire rack. Decorate as desired. Yield: 5 dozen.

Norwegian Butter Knots

Now where have we seen this shape before?

4 egg yolks
1 cup sugar   ¹/₂ cup sour cream
¹/₂ teaspoon baking soda
1 teaspoon vanilla or almond extract
1 cup butter
4 cups flour
4 egg whites, beaten
Coarsely crushed loaf sugar

Beat egg yolks and 1 cup sugar in bowl. Add mixture of sour cream, baking soda and flavoring; mix well. Cut butter into flour in bowl until crumbly. Add sour cream mixture; mix well. Divide into small portions. Roll each into small rope; shape into knot. Dip into beaten egg white; coat with coarse sugar. Place on lightly greased cookie sheet. Bake at 350 degrees until golden brown. Cool on wire rack. Yield: 4 dozen.

German Pfefferneusse

These "peppernuts" can be made as small as peanuts, aged in cheesecloth sacks for several weeks to dry and crisp, and served for crunchy snacks.

3½ cups flour
2 teaspoons baking soda
1 teaspoon cinnamon
1 teaspoon cloves   1 teaspoon ginger
1 cup margarine, softened
1½ cups sugar   1 egg, beaten
2 tablespoons light corn syrup
½ teaspoon oil of anise

Sift flour, baking soda, cinnamon, cloves and ginger together. Cream margarine and sugar in mixer bowl until light and fluffy. Beat in egg, corn syrup and oil of anise. Add half the dry ingredients; mix well. Knead in remaining dry ingredients. Chill in airtight container overnight or longer. Roll into thin ropes; slice ½ inch thick with sharp knife. Place on cookie sheet. Bake at 350 degrees for 7 minutes. Remove to wire rack to cool. May roll out and cut with thimble if preferred. Yield: 20 servings.

English Shortbread

*Definitely **not** a bread.*

2 cups butter, softened
1 cup fine sugar
3 cups flour   1 cup cornstarch
1 teaspoon salt

Cream butter and sugar in bowl until blended. Add mixture of flour, cornstarch and salt gradually to butter mixture, mixing well after each addition. Knead until smooth on floured surface. Press into 10½x15½-inch baking pan. Roll until smooth. Score into 2-inch squares. Prick with fork. Chill thoroughly. Cut into squares. Place on cookie sheet. Bake at 275 degrees for 30 minutes or until light brown. Place in airtight container. Yield: 3 dozen.

How can such a delicious, satisfying treat as a chocolate truffle be named after a mushroom? Possibly because the mushroom truffle is such a treasure! Unlike the mushroom we all recognize in the supermarket, truffles cannot be tamed. They are found only in the woods— detected by pigs trained to detect their delicate smell under the ground and then harvested painstakingly to be lovingly prepared and savored. Make your truffles with care and a light touch and place each cocoa-coated candy in a tiny paper bonbon cup. Be prepared to enjoy a rare and heavenly experience.

Chocolate Truffles

(English Version)

6 ounces semisweet baking chocolate
10 tablespoons butter, softened
2 egg yolks, beaten
1¹/₂ cups sifted confectioners' sugar
2 teaspoons vanilla extract
Baking cocoa

Melt chocolate in saucepan over very low heat, stirring constantly. Cool. Cream butter with egg yolks in mixer bowl. Add confectioners' sugar gradually, blending well after each addition. Stir in chocolate and vanilla. Chill until firm enough to handle. Shape into 30 to 35 balls. Roll in cocoa. Store in airtight container. Yield: 30 to 35 truffles.

Truffes au Chocolat

(French Translation)

6 onces de chocolat demi-sucré
10 cuillerées à soupe de beurre, ramolli
2 jaunes d'œuf, battus
1½ tasses de sucre glace
2 cuillerées à café d'extrait de vanille
Du cacao

Faites fondre le chocolat dans une casserole sur un feu très doux en remuant constamment. Faites refroidir. Mélangez dans un bol le beurre avec les jaunes d'œuf. Ajoutez petit à petit le sucre; mélangez bien. Ajoutez le chocolat et la vanille. Mettez au réfrigérator jusqu'à ce que le mélange soit ferme. Formez en 30 à 35 boules. Roulez dans du cacao. Conservez dans un récipient bien fermé. Pour 30 à 35 truffes.

Schokoladentrüffel

(German Translation)

6 Unzen halbbittere Schokolade zum Backen
10 Eßlöffel erweichte Butter
2 Eigelb, geschlagen
1½ Tassen gesiebten Konditoreizucker
2 Teelöffel Vanilleextrakt
Kakao

Schokolade in einem Saucentopf bei sehr schwacher Hitze unter ständigem Umrühren schmelzen. Abkühlen lassen. Butter mit Eigelb in einer Schüssel cremig schlagen. Nach und nach Konditoreizucker hinzufügen, gut mischen. Schokolade und Vanille hinzumischen. Kalt stellen bis die Masse fest genug ist, sie zu formen. Zu 30 bis 35 kleine Kugeln formen. In Kakao rollen. In einem luftdichten Behälter aufbewahren. Ergibt 30 bis 35 Trüffel.

Tartufi di cioccolata

(Italian Translation)

6 once cioccolata agrodolce
10 cucchiai burro ammorbidito
2 rossi di uovo, sbattuti
1¹/₂ tazze zucchero in polvere
2 cucchiaini vaniglia
Cacao

Sciogliere la cioccolata in pentola su fuoco molto lento, girando costantemente. Rinfrescare. Sbattere il burro con i rossi di uovo in scodella. Aggiungere lo zucchero gradualmente, mescolando bene. Aggiungere la cioccolata e la vaniglia. Raffreddare finché abbastanza duro da manipolare. Formare in 30 a 35 palline. Rotolare in cacao. Conservare in scatola a tenuta d'aria. Porzioni: 30 a 35.

Trufas de chocolate

(Spanish Translation)

6 onzas de chocolate de cocina, dulciamargo
10 cucharadas de mantequilla ablandada
2 yemas de huevo, batidas
1¹/₂ tazas de azúcar
2 cucharaditas de concentrado de vainilla
Cacao

Derretir el chocolate en una olla puesta a fuego lentísimo, revolviéndole de vez en cuando. Dejar enfriarse. Formar nata con la mantequilla y las yemas de huevo, en una fuente. Agregarle lentamente el azúcar a esta nata, revolviéndola bien. Agregarle el chocolate y el concentrado de vainilla, revolviendo la mezcla al mismo tiempo. Refrigerar hasta cuajarse lo suficiente para manejarse. Formar de 30 a 35 bolitas. Arrollarse en el cacao para que se rocien de él. Guardarse en un envase bien sellado. Rendimiento: 30 o 35 trufas.

French Marzipan

1 egg white   1 cup almond paste
1¹/₂ cups (about) confectioners' sugar
Lemon juice   Paste or liquid food coloring

Beat egg white in bowl until frothy. Add almond paste gradually. Add enough confectioners' sugar gradually to make paste easy to handle. Add lemon juice 1 drop at a time if necessary to make of desired consistency. Shape into any fruit or other shapes as desired. Knead in paste food coloring or paint with diluted liquid food coloring if desired. Glaze paste candies with solution of gum arabic. Yield: 1 dozen.

Strawberries: Tint, shape and texturize on small grater. Add cloves and angelica for stems.

Bananas: Tint, shape and paint markings with brown food coloring.

Oranges: Proceed as for strawberries.

Apples and Pears: Tint, shape and paint blossom end brown. Add blush and cloves for stems.

Grapes: Tint, shape and arrange in cluster.

English Toffee

1 cup butter   1 cup sugar
1 teaspoon light corn syrup
1 cup finely chopped almonds
Salt to taste   ¹/₈ teaspoon baking soda
16 ounces milk chocolate, melted
1 cup chopped walnuts

Combine butter, sugar, corn syrup, almonds and salt in saucepan. Cook over low heat until sugar is completely dissolved, stirring constantly. Cook over medium heat to 300 to 310 degrees on candy thermometer, hard-crack stage; do not stir. Remove from heat. Stir in baking soda. Spread half the melted chocolate over bottom of 9x13-inch dish lined with buttered foil. Pour toffee into prepared dish. Let stand until firm. Spread remaining chocolate over top. Sprinkle with walnuts. Let stand until set. Break into pieces. Yield: 2¹/₂ pounds.

Dumpling—what an interesting word. Have you eaten chicken and dumplings, or blackberry dumplings or been called someone's precious dumpling? Dumplings can be lumps of dough or noodle-like strips cooked in savory broth or syrupy fruit juices, but these apple dumplings are quite different—more like individual apple pies. Whether the crust is made of pie pastry, puff pastry, phyllo or thinly rolled biscuit dough, we recommend that you double the recipe.

Apple Dumplings

(English Version)

1 package frozen puff pastry, thawed
4 large cooking apples
$1/4$ cup chopped almonds
$1/4$ cup raisins
4 teaspoons sugar
4 teaspoons red currant jelly
1 egg, beaten

Roll puff pastry dough very thin on lightly floured surface. Cut into 4 squares large enough to wrap around apples. Peel and core apples. Place 1 apple in center of each pastry square. Fill apple centers with almonds, raisins, sugar and jelly. Fold pastry to cover apple. Moisten edges; press together at top to seal. Prick with fork. Place on buttered baking sheet. Brush with beaten egg. Bake at 350 degrees for 45 minutes or until pastry begins to sag as apples become tender. Serve warm with vanilla sauce or ice cream.
Yield: 4 servings.

Chaussons de Pomme

(French Translation)

1 bloc de pâte feuilletée, dégelée
4 grandes pommes   ¹⁄₂ tasse d'amandes hachées
¹⁄₄ tasse de raisins secs   4 cuillerées à café de sucre semoule
4 cuillerées à café de confiture de groseilles   1 œuf, battu

Préchauffez le four à 350 degés. Étalez la pâte au rouleau sur une planche farinée. Découpez-la en 4 carrés, chacun assez grand pour couvrir une pomme. Pelez les pommes et otez la partie centrale et les pépins. Mettez une pomme au centre de chaque carré de pâte. Remplissez le centre de chaque pomme avec un mélange des amandes, des raisins secs, du sucre et de la confiture. Repliez les bords de la pâte de façon à envelopper complètement la pomme, en les pinçant pour les sceller. Mettez-les sur un plat allant au four préalablement beurré. Badigeonnez-les avec l'œuf battu. Faites cuire au four pendant 45 minutes ou jusqu'à ce que la pâte soit légèrement dorée et les pommes tendres. Servez-les chaudes avec de la sauce à vanille ou de la glace. Pour 4 personnes.

Apfel im Schlafrock

(German Translation)

1 Packung gefrorener Blätterteig, aufgetaut
4 große Kochäpfel   ¹⁄₄ Tasse gehackte Mandeln
¹⁄₄ Tasse Rosinen   4 Teelöffel Zucker
4 Teelöffel Johannisbeergelee   1 Ei, geschlagen

Den Backofen auf 350 Grad vorheizen. Den Blätterteig auf leicht mit Mehl bestäubter Oberfläche sehr dünn ausrollen. In 4 Quadrate schneiden; jedes Quadrat muß groß genug für jeweils einen Apfel sein. Die Äpfel schälen und vom Kerngehäuse befreien. Jeweils 1 Apfel in die Mitte eines Teig-Quadrats legen; die Äpfel mit den Mandeln, Rosinen, dem Zucker und Gelee füllen. Den Teig über den Äpfeln zusammenfalten. Ecken befeuchten und oben gut zusammenpressen. Mit einer Gabel anstechen. Auf ein mit Butter ausgestrichenes Backblech geben. Mit dem geschlagenen Ei bestreichen. 45 Minuten backen oder bis der Teig etwas zusammensinkt (die Äpfel sind dann gar). Warm mit Vanillesoße oder mit Eis Servieren. Ergibt 4 Portionen.

Dolci di mela

(Italian Translation)

1 libbra pasta sfoglia   4 grandi mele
¹/₄ tazza mandorle tritate   ¹/₄ tazza uva secche
4 cucchiaini zucchero
4 cucchiaini conserva di ribes   1 uovo, sbattuto

Accendere il forno a 350 gradi. Stendere la pasta finché molto sottile su un tavolo infarinato. Tagliare in 4 pezzi abbastanza grandi da coprire le mele. Sbucciare e estrarre il torsolo dalle mele. Mettere una mela nel centro di ogni quadro di pasta. Riempire i centri delle mele con le mandorle, le uva secche, lo zucchero e la conserva. Piegare la pasta per coprire la mela. Umettare i margini della pasta e premere insieme. Pungere con una forchetta. Mettere su una teglia imburrata e spazzolare con l'uovo. Cuocere 45 minuti o finché la pasta comincia a piegarsi quando le mele comincino ad ammorbidirsi. Servire calde con salsa di vaniglia o gelato. Porzioni: 4.

Pastelitos de manzana

(Spanish Translation)

1 paquete de hojas congeladas de masa para pasteles
hinchados: descongelarse
4 manzanas grandes   ¹/₄ taza de almendras picadas
¹/₄ taza de pasas   4 cucharaditas de azúcar
4 cucharadas de mermelada de grosella roja   1 huevo batido

Calentarse el horno a 350 grados. Extenderse la masa con el rodillo sobre una superficie rociada ligeramente con harina. Cortarse en 4 hojas de tamaño suficientemente grante para forrar las manzanas. Pelar las manzanas, y quitarles el corazón. Colocar una manzana en el centro de cada hoja de masa. Rellenar cada manzana de almendras, pasas, azúcar y mermelada. Sellar la manzana dentro de la masa. Mojar los márgenes de la hoja y apretarlos para sellarse. Pinchar la hoja con un tenedor. Ponerse sobre una chapa engrasada con mante-quilla. Aplicarse el huevo a los pasteles con una brocha. Cocinar al horno por 45 minutos, o hasta que el pastel empiece a hundirse mientras la manzana se ponga tierna. Servirse tibio el pastel, con salsa o helado de vainilla. Rendimiento: 4 porciones.

Dutch Apple Pie

4 cups sliced peeled apples
1 cup sugar
1 teaspoon cinnamon
2 tablespoons flour
1/2 teaspoon salt
1 unbaked 9-inch pie shell
1/2 cup oats
2/3 cup melted butter or margarine
1 1/2 cups packed light brown sugar
1 1/2 cups flour
1/2 teaspoon baking soda

Combine apples, sugar, cinnamon, 2 tablespoons flour and salt in bowl; mix well. Place in pie shell. Mix oats, butter, brown sugar, remaining 1 1/2 cups flour and baking soda in bowl. Sprinkle over pie. Bake at 350 degrees for 45 to 60 minutes or until apples are tender. May wrap foil around edge of pie shell before baking to prevent burning. Yield: 8 servings.

Streusel-Topped Apple Pie

(German)

3 cups sliced apples
1 unbaked 9-inch pie shell   2 eggs, beaten
1   14-ounce can sweetened condensed milk
1/4 cup melted butter
1/2 teaspoon cinnamon   Dash of nutmeg
1/4 cup cold butter
1/2 cup packed light brown sugar
1/2 cup flour   1/2 cup chopped nuts

Arrange apples in pie shell. Add mixture of eggs, condensed milk, 1/4 cup melted butter, cinnamon and nutmeg. Cut cold butter into brown sugar and flour in bowl until crumbly. Stir in nuts. Sprinkle over apples. Bake at 425 degrees for 10 minutes. Reduce temperature to 375 degrees. Bake for 35 minutes longer. Chill in refrigerator. Yield: 6 servings.

Greek Baklava

2 pounds honey, warmed   1 pound phyllo dough
1 pound butter, melted   1¾ to 2 pounds walnuts, crushed
Cinnamon   Cloves

Reserve about ⅓ of the honey. Layer 5 sheets phyllo in buttered 9x13-inch baking pan, brushing each sheet with butter. Add generous sprinkle of walnuts, drizzle of honey and sprinkle of cinnamon and cloves. Repeat with remaining ingredients, ending with phyllo. Cut layers into 36 diamond-shaped pieces with sharp knife. Bake at 350 degrees for 20 minutes or until light brown. Drizzle half the reserved honey over top, prick with fork and drizzle with remaining honey. Flavor improves if made day before serving. Yield: 36 pieces.

Banana Wellington

Always cover unused phyllo with damp cloth to prevent drying when making this delicious English dessert.

1   10-ounce package frozen raspberries in light syrup, thawed
1 tablespoon sugar   1 teaspoon cornstarch
2 firm ripe bananas   8   12x17-inch sheets phyllo dough
½ cup coarsely chopped white chocolate
½ cup toasted sliced almonds   Vegetable oil for frying
Confectioners' sugar

Purée raspberries, sugar and cornstarch in blender. Strain into saucepan. Cook over medium heat for 5 minutes or until thickened, stirring constantly. Chill in refrigerator. Cut bananas into halves; cut each half lengthwise. Fold each phyllo sheet in half crosswise. Place 1 banana piece in center. Sprinkle with 1 tablespoon white chocolate and 1 tablespoon almonds. Brush edges of dough with water. Fold sides to center; roll up from short end, pressing edge to seal. Heat 1 inch oil to 325 degrees in large heavy saucepan. Fry 4 phyllo rolls at a time for 3 to 4 minutes or until golden brown, turning to brown evenly. Drain on paper towels. Keep warm in oven. Place phyllo rolls on dessert plates. Spoon raspberry sauce over rolls. Garnish with confectioners' sugar. Serve hot. Yield: 8 servings.

French Bombe Glacé

3 pints lime sherbet, softened
1 pint chocolate or vanilla ice cream, softened
2 pints raspberry sherbet, softened
1 cup whipping cream
2 tablespoons sugar
Frosted grapes

Spread lime sherbet evenly in 8-cup round mold. Freeze until firm. Spread ice cream evenly over lime sherbet. Freeze until firm. Fill mold to rim with raspberry sherbet. Freeze until firm. Place mold in cold water for several seconds. Loosen edge with knife. Invert onto serving plate. Return to freezer. Whip cream in mixer bowl until soft peaks form. Add sugar; mix well. Spoon into pastry tube. Pipe rosettes around base of bombe. Pipe rosettes in a cross from base to base across top. Pipe rosette cluster on top. Freeze until serving time. Garnish with frosted grapes.
Yield: 16 servings.

Russian Cheese Blintz

2 egg whites   2 eggs
1 cup plus 3 tablespoons flour
1¹/₃ cups milk   ¹/₂ teaspoon salt
¹/₄ cup melted butter
7 tablespoons (about) vegetable oil
3 pounds hoop cheese   1 cup cottage cheese
4 egg yolks   1 cup white raisins
¹/₂ cup sugar   2 teaspoons salt
¹/₂ cup butter   1 cup sour cream

Combine egg whites, eggs, flour, milk, ¹/₂ teaspoon salt and ¹/₄ cup butter in mixer bowl; beat well. Pour 1 ladlefull batter into 1 teaspoon hot oil in crêpe pan. Tilt to coat pan. Cook over medium heat until brown. Repeat with remaining batter. Combine hoop cheese, cottage cheese, egg yolks, raisins, sugar and remaining 2 teaspoons salt in bowl; mix well. Place 2 tablespoons cheese mixture on each crêpe. Roll to enclose filling. Brown in ¹/₂ cup butter in skillet; remove to serving plate. Top with sour cream.
Yield: 18 to 20 servings.

Here is a chocolate cake like none other. It could be called a special diet cake for those allergic to flour, but the magic is in the ultra smooth texture, the melt-in-your-mouth goodness and the rich satisfying flavor. Do not attempt to use semisweet chocolate chips which contain additives. Blocks of pure semisweet chocolate make this heavenly foolproof dessert a royal treat.

Flourless Chocolate Cake

(English Version)

7 ounces semisweet chocolate
1/2 cup butter
1 cup sugar
7 eggs, separated

Melt chocolate and butter in saucepan over low heat, stirring constantly. Pour into mixer bowl. Add sugar gradually, beating constantly. Add egg yolks 1 at a time, beating well after each addition. Beat egg whites in mixer bowl until stiff peaks form. Fold into chocolate mixture gently. Pour 3/4 of the batter into ungreased 8-inch springform pan. Bake at 325 degrees for 35 minutes. Let stand until cool; cake will fall. Loosen cake from side of pan with knife. Remove side of pan. Spoon remaining batter over top. Chill until serving time. Garnish with whipped cream and chocolate shavings. Yield: 10 servings.

Gâteau au Chocolat sans Farine

(French Translation)

**7 onces de chocolat demi-sucré   ½ tasse de beurre
1 tasse de sucre semoule   7 œufs**

Faites fondre le chocolat et le beurre dans une casserole sur feu doux, tout en remuant constamment. Versez-le dans une terrine. Ajoutez le sucre petit à petit. Cassez les œufs en réservant les blancs. Ajoutez les jaunes d'œuf, un par un, au mélange de chocolat; mélangez bien après chaque addition. Montez les blancs d'œufs en neige dans un bol à mixer à l'aide d'un fouet électrique. Incorporez délicatement le chocolat aux blancs en neige. Garnissez de ¾ de cette préparation un moule à manqué. Mettez au four à 375 degrés. pendant 35 minutes. Laissez le gâteau refroidir et démoulez-le. Nappez avec le reste de la préparation chocolat. Mettez-le au froid jusqu'à l'heure de servir. Garnissez-le avec de la crème Chantilly et des morceaux fins de chocolat.
Pour 10 personnes.

Mehlloser Schokoladekuchen

(German Translation)

**7 Unzen halbbittere Schokolade   ½ Tasse Butter
1 Tasse Zucker   7 Eier, getrennt**

Schokolade und Butter bei niedriger Hitze in einem Saucentopf unter ständigem Rühren schmelzen. In Mixschüssel gießen. Nach und nach Zucker zufügen, dabei die Masse ständig schlagen. Jeweils ein Eigelb hinzufügen, nach jedem Hinzufügen gut vermischen. Eiweiß in Mixschüssel zu festem Eischnee schlagen. Vorsichtig unter die Schokoladenmischung geben. ¾ des Teiges in eine ungefettete ca 20cm große Springform gießen. Bei 325 Grad Fahrenheit 35 Minuten lang backen. Stehen lassen bis abgekühlt; der Kuchen wird zusammenfallen. Den Kuchen vom Rand der Form mit Messer ablösen. Das Seitenteil der Kuchenform abnehmen. Den restlichen Teig über den Kuchen geben. Bis zum Servieren kalt stellen. Mit Schlagsahne und Schokoladenraspeln garnieren. Ergiebt 10 Stücke.

Torta di cioccolata senza farina

(Italian Translation)

7 once cioccolata agrodolce
1/2 tazza burro   1 tazza zucchero
7 uova, separate

Sciogliere la cioccolata e il burro in una pentola a fuoco lento, girando costantemente. Versare in scodella. Aggiungere lo zucchero gradualmente, sbattendo costantemente. Aggiungere i rossi di uovo uno alla volta, sbattendo bene dopo ogni addizione. Montare i bianchi di uovo. Mescolare lievemente con la cioccolata. Versare 3/4 della pastella in una pentola da torta di 8 pollici, non imburrata. Cuocere a 325 gradi 35 minuti. Rinfrescare in pentola. Liberare i lati della torta con coltello e rimuovere i lati della pentola. Versare il resto della pastella sulla torta. Mettere al freddo. Servire con panna montata e cioccolata grattata. Porzioni: 10.

Torta de chocolate sin harina

(Spanish Translation)

7 onzas de chocolate dulciamargo
1/2 taza de mantequilla   1 taza de azúcar
7 huevos, separada la yema de la clara

Derretir el chocolate y la mantequilla en una olla puesta a fuego lento. Agregar lentamente el azúcar, revolviendo constantemente la mezcla. Echarse, una por una, las yemas de huevo en esta mezcla, revolviendo bien la mezcla después de echarle cada yema. Batir en una fuente las claras de huevo hasta formarse picos. Echar suavemente las claras de huevo batidas en la mezcla de chocolate. Echar tres cuartos de la pasta en una cacerola para tortas (de las que se les puede quitar el costado de la base) de 8 pulgadas, no engrasada. Cocinar al horno a 325 grados por 35 minutos. Dejar enfriarse; el centro de la torta se hundirá. Separar la torta de los costados de la cacerola con un cuchillo. Quitarle el costado a la base de la cacerola. Echar la pasta que ha quedado sin cocerse encima de la torta ya cocida. Dejar enfriarse hasta la hora de servirse. Adornar con nata batida y virutas de chocolate. Rendimiento: 10 porciones.

Black Forest Cake

*The original **German** version of this cake is multilayered, beautiful and sumptuous, but this shortcut version has everything but the time involved. If calories aren't important, add your favorite chocolate frosting and garnish with lots of whipped cream.*

1 2-layer package chocolate cake mix
1 21-ounce can cherry pie filling
2 eggs
1 teaspoon vanilla extract
Whipped cream

Combine cake mix, pie filling, eggs and vanilla in bowl; mix well. Pour into 1 greased and floured 9x13-inch cake pan or 2 layer cake pans. Bake using package directions. Cool. Frost generously with whipped cream. Yield: 8 to 12 servings.

Mexican Chocolate Cake

Another shortcut triumph. Don't omit the cinnamon—it is necessary to the Mexican character.

1 2-layer package chocolate cake mix
1¹/₂ to 2 teaspoons cinnamon
¹/₂ cup butter
2 ounces unsweetened chocolate
6 tablespoons milk
1 pound confectioners' sugar
1 teaspoon vanilla extract
1 to 1¹/₂ cups chopped nuts

Prepare cake mix using package directions, adding cinnamon. Pour into 12x15-inch cake pan. Bake at 350 degrees for 20 minutes or until cake tests done. Heat butter, chocolate and milk in saucepan until bubbles form around edge of pan; remove from heat. Add confectioners' sugar, vanilla and nuts; mix well. Spread over warm cake. Yield: 16 to 18 servings.

French Cream Puff Ring

1 cup water   1/2 cup butter or margarine
1 cup flour   4 eggs
2 cups milk   2 cups sour cream
2 4-ounce packages French vanilla instant pudding mix
1/2 teaspoon vanilla extract
1 21-ounce can cherry pie filling

Bring water and butter to a boil in 1-quart saucepan. Stir in flour. Cook for 1 minute or until mixture forms a ball, stirring vigorously. Remove from heat. Add eggs. Beat at low speed with electric mixer for 2 minutes or until smooth. Drop by tablespoonfuls onto greased baking sheet to form 8-inch ring. Smooth with spatula. Bake at 400 degrees for 50 to 60 minutes or until puffed and golden brown. Cool on baking sheet for several minutes. Remove to wire rack to cool completely. Cut top off cream puff ring; remove any soft dough inside. Combine milk and sour cream in mixer bowl; mix well. Add pudding mix and vanilla; beat well. Place cream puff ring on serving plate. Fill with pudding mixture. Spoon half the pie filling over pudding. Replace top. Spoon remaining pie filling over all. Chill until serving time. Yield: 15 servings.

Chocolate Pain Perdu

(French)

5 tablespoons butter, softened
12 slices French bread   1 cup semisweet chocolate chips
2 1/2 cups milk   1/4 cup dry milk powder
3 eggs   1/4 cup sugar   1 teaspoon cinnamon
2 tablespoons confectioners' sugar

Butter bread on both sides. Place on baking sheet. Bake at 375 degrees until golden brown on both sides, turning once. Arrange in 9x13-inch baking dish. Melt chocolate chips with 1/2 cup milk in saucepan. Scald remaining 2 cups milk with milk powder in saucepan. Stir in chocolate mixture. Beat eggs with sugar and cinnamon in mixer bowl. Stir in milk mixture. Pour over bread. Bake at 350 degrees for 40 minutes or until set. Sprinkle with confectioners' sugar. Serve warm with cream. Yield: 12 servings.

French Almond Crêpes

1/3 cup flour   1 tablespoon sugar
Dash of salt
1 egg   1 egg yolk   3/4 cup milk
1 tablespoon melted butter
Almond Cream Filling
Grated unsweetened chocolate
Confectioners' sugar

Beat flour, sugar, salt, egg, egg yolk, milk and 1 tablespoon melted butter in mixer bowl until smooth. Chill for several hours or until thickened. Heat heavy 6-inch skillet; grease lightly. Add 2 tablespoons batter. Lift skillet from heat; tilt from side to side until batter covers bottom evenly. Return to heat. Cook for 1½ minutes or until underside of crêpe is light brown. Invert onto paper towels. Repeat. Spread about 2 tablespoons Almond Cream Filling on unbrowned side of each crêpe. Roll up to enclose filling. Place folded side down in buttered 9x13-inch baking dish. Brush crêpes with additional melted butter. Bake at 350 degrees for 20 to 25 minutes. Sprinkle with grated unsweetened chocolate. Sift confectioners' sugar over all. Serve warm with whipped cream. Yield: 4 servings.

Almond Cream Filling

1 cup sugar   1/4 cup flour
1 cup milk   2 eggs
2 egg yolks
3 tablespoons butter
2 teaspoons vanilla extract
1/2 teaspoon almond extract
1/2 cup ground toasted blanched almonds

Mix sugar and flour together in saucepan. Add milk. Cook until thickened, stirring constantly. Cook for 1 or 2 minutes longer, stirring constantly. Beat eggs and egg yolks in bowl slightly. Stir a small amount of hot mixture into eggs; stir eggs into hot mixture. Bring just to a boil, stirring constantly; remove from heat. Stir in butter and flavorings. Add ground almonds; mix well. Cool to room temperature. Yield: 3 cups.

Chocolate Chocolate Crêpes

*Try substituting coffee, chocolate chips or peppermint ice cream in these exquisite **French** crêpes. What a great idea for a party! Let the guests build their own.*

1/2 cup semisweet chocolate chips
2 tablespoons butter or margarine
1/2 cup sifted confectioners' sugar
1/4 cup light corn syrup
2 tablespoons water
1/2 teaspoon vanilla extract
1 quart chocolate ice cream
Chocolate Crêpes
1/2 cup chopped pecans

Melt chocolate chips and butter in double boiler; mix well. Remove from heat. Stir in confectioners' sugar, corn syrup, water and vanilla. Spoon 3 tablespoons ice cream down center of each crêpe; fold sides over to enclose. Place seam side down on serving plates. Top with warm chocolate sauce; sprinkle with pecans. Yield: 10 servings.

Chocolate Crêpes

1/2 cup flour
1 tablespoon baking cocoa
2 teaspoons sugar
Dash of salt
3/4 cup milk
1/4 teaspoon almond extract
1 egg
2 teaspoons melted butter or margarine

Mix flour, cocoa, sugar and salt in bowl. Add milk and almond extract; beat until smooth. Beat in egg. Stir in butter. Chill for 2 hours. Spoon 2 tablespoons batter at a time into hot oiled crêpe pan; tilt pan. Cook for 1 minute or until light brown. Turn crêpe. Cook for 30 seconds. Cool. Stack between layers of waxed paper. Yield: ten 6-inch crêpes.

Viennese Crêpes

3 eggs   1 cup milk
1 tablespoon sugar
1½ cups flour
1 cup club soda
1   20-ounce can sliced apples, drained, chopped
2 cups sour cream
3 cups shredded Swiss cheese

Beat eggs with milk, sugar and flour in mixer bowl. Let stand at room temperature for 30 minutes. Stir in club soda. Spoon 2 tablespoons at a time into heated 7-inch crêpe pan which has been lightly brushed with butter; swirl to spread evenly. Bake for 2 to 3 minutes or until light brown on bottom. Turn crêpe. Bake until light brown. Stack crêpes on plate and keep warm in 300-degree oven. Combine apples with sour cream in bowl. Spoon 2 tablespoons apple mixture onto each crêpe; top with 2 tablespoons cheese. Roll crêpes to enclose filling. Place in buttered 9x13-inch baking dish. Spoon remaining apple mixture evenly around crêpes; sprinkle with remaining cheese. Bake at 350 degrees for 10 minutes or until heated through. Yield: 16 servings.

South Seas Fruit Bake

½ cup packed brown sugar   ¼ cup butter, melted
1 teaspoon grated lemon rind
2 tablespoons lemon juice   ⅛ teaspoon nutmeg
3 bananas   1 papaya
1 cup honeydew melon balls
1 cup cantaloupe balls
Flaked coconut

Combine brown sugar, butter, lemon rind, lemon juice and nutmeg in bowl; mix well. Peel bananas; cut into halves crosswise and lengthwise. Peel papaya; discard seed and cube fruit. Combine all fruit in bowl; divide among 6 squares of heavy-duty foil. Sprinkle with brown sugar mixture and coconut. Seal foil to make tight packages. Place on grill rack over hot coals. Grill for 10 to 15 minutes or until heated through. Yield: 6 servings.

Quiche Alsacienne aux Fruits

(French)

3 tablespoons butter
2 pounds tart apples, peeled, quartered
1 tablespoon sugar   2 eggs   1 egg yolk
1/2 cup sugar   1/4 cup milk
6 tablespoons heavy cream
1/2 teaspoon vanilla extract   1 recipe 1-crust pie pastry
1   12-ounce jar apricot jam
Juice of 1/2 lemon   2 to 3 tablespoons water

Melt butter in skillet. Add apples; sprinkle with 1 tablespoon sugar. Cook over medium heat until apples are almost caramelized and tender, shaking skillet occasionally. Beat eggs, egg yolk and 1/2 cup sugar in bowl. Stir in milk, cream and vanilla. Line 12-inch pie plate with pastry; prick with fork. Arrange apples in prepared pie plate; pour egg mixture over top. Place on hot baking sheet on bottom rack of oven. Bake at 400 degrees for 30 to 40 minutes or until set. Remove to wire rack to cool. Melt jam with lemon juice and enough water to make glaze in non-aluminum saucepan. Pour through strainer. Brush quiche with 1/3 cup glaze. May prepare 1 day ahead. Yield: 6 to 8 servings.

Cold German Fruit Soup

1 cantaloupe
1   21-ounce can cherry pie filling, chilled
1 teaspoon ground cinnamon
Pinch of ground cloves   1/2 cup cold orange juice
2 whole cinnamon sticks
1 can instant whipped cream

Pare cantaloupe carefully. Slice melon neatly into halves. Remove pulp, seed and enough melon from center to hold soup. Place cherry pie filling, ground cinnamon, cloves and orange juice in blender container. Blend at high speed for 1 minute or until smooth. Pour cherry-orange mixture into cantaloupe shells. Decorate each with cinnamon stick and whipped cream. Serve immediately. Yield: 2 servings.

Grecian Galatobourika

3 cups milk   1 cup sugar
1/2 cup cream of wheat
4 eggs, at room temperature
1 tablespoon butter or margarine
1 teaspoon vanilla extract   1 pound phyllo dough
2 cups melted butter or margarine
3 cups water   2 1/2 cups sugar
1 cinnamon stick   1 cup honey

Combine milk, 1 cup sugar, cream of wheat and eggs in saucepan; mix well. Cook over medium heat until thickened, stirring constantly. Remove from heat. Stir in 1 tablespoon butter and vanilla. Cool. Separate phyllo dough sheets; brush with melted butter. Layer phyllo dough in 8x8-inch baking dish to 1/4-inch thickness. Spread cream of wheat filling over dough. Cover with layers of buttered phyllo dough to 1/4-inch thickness. Bake at 350 degrees for 20 minutes or until brown. Combine water, remaining 2 1/2 cups sugar and cinnamon stick in saucepan. Cook for 30 minutes or until thickened, stirring frequently. Remove cinnamon stick. Stir in honey. Pour over hot Galatobourika. Yield: 12 to 16 servings.

Fried Mexican Ice Cream

1 pint ice cream
1/2 cup crushed cornflakes or cookie crumbs
1 teaspoon cinnamon   2 teaspoons sugar
1 egg   Oil for deep frying
Honey   Whipped cream

Scoop 4 or 5 balls of ice cream into bowl. Place in freezer. Mix crumbs, cinnamon and sugar in bowl. Roll ice cream balls in half the crumb mixture; return to freezer. Beat egg in bowl. Dip ice cream balls in egg; roll in remaining crumbs. Return to freezer. Preheat oil to 350 degrees in deep-fryer. Place 1 ice cream ball in deep-fryer basket. Deep-fry for 1 minute. Remove to dessert compote. Drizzle with honey; top with whipped cream. Repeat with remaining ice cream balls. Yield: 4 to 5 servings.

Maraschino Bavarian Cream

1   8-ounce jar red maraschino cherries
1 envelope unflavored gelatin   4 egg yolks
1/2 cup sugar   1/4 teaspoon salt   2 cups milk, scalded
2 drops of red food coloring
2 teaspoons vanilla extract   1 1/2 cups whipping cream
1 tablespoon sugar   Stemmed red maraschino cherries

Drain cherries, reserving 1/4 cup syrup. Chop cherries coarsely; drain on paper towels. Set aside. Soften gelatin in reserved syrup. Beat egg yolks in saucepan until light. Add 1/2 cup sugar and salt. Blend in milk gradually. Bring to a boil over low heat, stirring constantly; remove from heat. Add food coloring, gelatin and 1 1/2 teaspoons vanilla; stir until gelatin dissolves. Let stand until cool. Chill until mixture mounds slightly when dropped from a spoon. Whip 1 cup cream until soft peaks form. Beat gelatin mixture until fluffy. Fold in whipped cream and chopped cherries. Pour into oiled 1-quart mold. Chill for 4 hours or until set. Unmold onto serving plate. Whip 1/2 cup cream with 1 tablespoon sugar and 1/2 teaspoon vanilla until soft peaks form. Spoon into center of gelatin mixture. Garnish with stemmed cherries. Yield: 6 to 8 servings.

Black and White Mousse

(French)

6 ounces white chocolate   1/2 cup light corn syrup
2 egg whites   1/4 cup sugar   1/2 cup sifted confectioners' sugar
2 cups whipping cream   1/2 teaspoon vanilla extract
8 ounces bittersweet chocolate   1/2 cup whipping cream

Melt white chocolate in saucepan over low heat; remove from heat. Stir in corn syrup. Beat egg whites until stiff. Beat in sugar gradually until very stiff. Fold in chocolate mixture gently. Beat confectioners' sugar, 2 cups cream and vanilla in bowl until soft peaks form. Fold in chocolate mixture gently. Pour into serving bowl. Chill, covered, for 4 to 24 hours. Melt chocolate in heavy saucepan over low heat. Cool slightly. Stir in 1/2 cup cream. Spoon onto serving plates. Top with mousse. Drizzle remaining chocolate sauce over mousse. Yield: 8 servings.

White Chocolate Mousse

(French)

12 ounces white chocolate
³/₄ cup milk   1 envelope unflavored gelatin
¹/₄ cup cold milk   1 teaspoon vanilla extract
4 egg whites, at room temperature
2 cups whipping cream   Dash of lemon juice
1 10-ounce package frozen raspberries

Melt white chocolate in ³/₄ cup milk in double boiler over hot not boiling water; mix well. Remove from heat. Soften gelatin in remaining ¹/₄ cup milk. Add to chocolate mixture; stir until very smooth. Blend in vanilla. Beat egg whites until stiff peaks form. Fold gently ¹/₃ at a time into chocolate mixture. Whip cream until soft peaks form. Fold with lemon juice into chocolate mixture. Pour into serving bowl. Chill for several hours. Purée raspberries in blender. Strain to remove seed. Chill in refrigerator. Spoon sauce over mousse to serve. Yield: 12 servings.

Australian Pavlova

4 egg whites   1¹/₂ cups sugar
1¹/₂ teaspoons cornstarch   2 teaspoons white vinegar
1 teaspoon vanilla extract   3 tablespoons boiling water
Whipped cream, ice cream, sherbet or sorbet
4 to 6 kiwifruit, sliced   Fresh strawberries
Mint sprigs

Combine egg whites, sugar, cornstarch, vinegar, vanilla and water in mixer bowl. Beat at high speed for 6 to 8 minutes or until very stiff peaks form. Spoon into 8-inch circle on greased baking parchment-lined baking sheet, building sides to form ring; hollow out center slightly. Bake at 350 degrees for 10 minutes. Reduce temperature to 300 degrees. Bake for 45 minutes longer or until meringue is crisp. Turn off oven. Let meringue stand in closed oven until cool. Place on serving plate. Fill with whipped cream. Top with kiwifruit. Garnish with strawberries and mint sprigs. Yield: 12 servings.

Mexican Capirotada

Bread pudding you won't believe.

1   15-ounce package raisins
2 cups packed dark brown sugar
1 tablespoon allspice
4 cups water
15 slices white bread, toasted
1 pound Monterey Jack cheese, shredded

Rinse raisins; drain. Combine brown sugar, allspice and water in saucepan. Simmer over medium heat for 5 to 10 minutes or until brown sugar is dissolved and mixture thickens, stirring constantly. Alternate layers of toasted bread, cheese and raisins in 3-quart casserole. Pour brown sugar mixture gradually over layers, soaking all bread. Use only amount of mixture needed. Bake bread pudding at 350 degrees for 30 minutes or until liquid is absorbed. Serve warm or cold. Store at room temperature. May add 1 cup peanuts and/or 1 cup coconut. Yield: 10 to 12 servings.

Cuban Flan

Custard with a touch of caramel.

Sugar
3 large eggs
1/2 teaspoon almond extract
1/2 cup evaporated milk
1   14-ounce can sweetened condensed milk
1 tablespoon water

Sprinkle sugar over bottom of metal mold. Cook over high heat until sugar is caramelized, stirring constantly. Cool to room temperature. Process eggs, almond extract, evaporated milk, condensed milk and water in blender at High speed for 2 minutes. Pour over caramelized sugar. Place mold in pan of water. Bake at 325 degrees for 20 to 25 minutes. Turn off oven. Let flan stand in oven for 2 hours or longer. Chill in refrigerator overnight. Unmold onto serving plate. Yield: 4 to 6 servings.

Flan de Coco

Mexican custard with coconut.

1 cup sugar
1 tablespoon water
1   14-ounce can sweetened condensed milk
1   12-ounce can evaporated milk
Grated meat of 1 coconut   6 eggs

Sprinkle sugar in heavy skillet. Stir in water. Cook over low heat for 8 to 10 minutes or until medium brown, stirring constantly with long-handled spoon. Pour into tube pan. Process condensed milk, evaporated milk, coconut and eggs in blender. Spoon carefully into prepared pan. Bake at 325 degrees for 1 hour. Invert immediately onto serving plate. Yield: 12 servings.

Crème Brûlée Amandine

French custard in another life?

2 cups whipping cream
7 egg yolks
1 teaspoon vanilla extract
1/3 cup packed light brown sugar
1/8 teaspoon salt
1/2 cup finely chopped toasted blanched almonds
3/4 cup packed light brown sugar

Scald whipping cream in double boiler. Remove from heat. Beat egg yolks in mixer bowl until thick and lemon-colored. Stir in vanilla, 1/3 cup brown sugar and salt. Add a small amount of hot cream to egg yolks. Stir egg yolks into hot cream. Cook over hot water to the consistency of mayonnaise, stirring constantly. Stir in almonds. Spoon into greased 8-inch round baking dish. Chill thoroughly. Sift remaining 3/4 cup brown sugar over top to about 1/4-inch thickness 2 hours before serving time. Broil for a few seconds or until brown sugar melts into an even glaze. Chill until serving time. Break through hard top crust with spoon to serve. Yield: 4 to 6 servings.

Raspberry-Peach Chantilly

(French)

2 packages frozen raspberries, thawed
4 tablespoons sifted confectioners' sugar
1 large can peach halves, chilled
1 cup whipping cream   1 teaspoon vanilla extract
1/4 cup chopped pistachios

Drain raspberries. Press raspberries through fine sieve using back of large spoon. Mix raspberry purée and 2 tablespoons confectioners' sugar in bowl. Chill, covered, in refrigerator. Drain peaches. Arrange peach halves in sherbet glasses; fill each peach half with raspberry mixture. Whip cream with remaining 2 tablespoons confectioners' sugar and vanilla until soft peaks form. Place whipped cream in pastry bag; pipe ring around each peach. Sprinkle pistachios over whipped cream. Yield: 6 to 8 servings.

Russian Blintz Soufflé

1 1/2 cups sour cream   1/2 cup orange juice
6 eggs   1/4 cup butter, softened
1 cup flour   1/3 cup sugar   2 teaspoons baking powder
16 ounces small curd cottage cheese
8 ounces cream cheese, softened
2 egg yolks, slightly beaten
1 tablespoon sugar   1 teaspoon vanilla extract
Apricot preserves   Sour cream

Combine sour cream, orange juice, eggs, butter, flour, 1/3 cup sugar and baking powder in blender container. Process until smooth, scraping sides often. Pour half the batter into greased 9x13-inch baking dish. Beat cottage cheese, cream cheese, egg yolks, remaining 1 tablespoon sugar and vanilla in mixer bowl until smooth. Drop by teaspoonfuls onto batter. Spread evenly; the 2 mixtures will blend slightly. Pour remaining batter over cottage cheese mixture. Chill, covered, for 2 hours to overnight. Bake, uncovered, at 350 degrees for 50 to 60 minutes or until puffy and light brown. Top with apricot preserves and sour cream. Yield: 12 servings.

Soufflé au Chocolat

French-style cold chocolate soufflé—cool, light, rich, delicious.

1 envelope unflavored gelatin
3 tablespoons cold water
2 ounces baking chocolate
1/2 cup confectioners' sugar
1 cup warm milk
3/4 cup sugar
1 teaspoon vanilla extract
1/4 teaspoon salt
2 cups whipping cream, whipped

Soften gelatin in cold water in bowl. Melt chocolate in saucepan over low heat. Blend in confectioners' sugar. Stir in warm milk gradually. Bring to a boil over low heat, stirring constantly; remove from heat. Stir in gelatin, sugar, vanilla and salt. Chill until slightly thickened. Beat with rotary beater until light and fluffy. Fold in whipped cream. Spoon into 2-quart serving dish. Chill for 2 hours or longer. Yield: 8 servings.

Chocolate Tortilla Torte

(Mexican)

1 cup semisweet chocolate chips
1 cup sour cream
1 tablespoon confectioners' sugar
4 flour tortillas
1 cup sour cream
2 tablespoons confectioners' sugar

Heat chocolate chips, 1 cup sour cream and 1 tablespoon confectioners' sugar in double boiler until chocolate chips melt; mix well. Cool in pan of cold water; stir occasionally. Spread mixture between tortillas. Spread mixture of 1 cup sour cream and 2 tablespoons confectioners' sugar over top and side of torte. Invert bowl over torte. Chill for 8 hours to overnight. Garnish with chocolate curls. Cut into wedges. Yield: 8 servings.

French Mocha Torte

1 cup butter, softened
1¹/₂ cups confectioners' sugar
Pinch of salt
1 teaspoon vanilla extract
2 ounces semisweet chocolate, melted
2 eggs, separated
6 tablespoons strong coffee
1 angel food cake
1 cup whipping cream, whipped
Chocolate sprinkles
Maraschino cherries

Cream butter, confectioners' sugar, salt and vanilla in mixer bowl until light and fluffy. Combine chocolate, egg yolks and coffee in small bowl. Add to creamed mixture; mix well. Beat egg whites until stiff peaks form. Fold gently into chocolate mixture. Split cake into 4 layers. Spread chocolate mixture between layers. Frost with whipped cream. Decorate with chocolate sprinkles and maraschino cherries. Yield: 12 servings.

Hungarian Nut Torte

2 cups flour
1 tablespoon baking powder
2 cups sugar
6 egg yolks
1 cup ground nuts
1 cup black coffee
1 teaspoon vanilla extract
6 egg whites, stiffly beaten

Combine flour, baking powder, sugar and egg yolks in bowl; mix well. Stir in nuts, coffee and vanilla. Fold in egg whites gently. Pour into greased and floured tube pan. Bake at 350 degrees for 45 minutes or until torte tests done. Remove to wire rack to cool. Spread with favorite frosting. Yield: 6 to 8 servings.

English Trifle

A trifle may be a synonym for a tiny amount with little importance but an English Trifle is a spectacular dessert of monumental proportions. Since at least half the enjoyment of a trifle is in the eye appeal, it is as carefully planned and executed as a painting. Trifles are traditionally prepared and served in straight-sided, footed glass bowls but a pretty punch bowl will serve the purpose.

6 egg yolks
2 ounces castor sugar
2 teaspoons cornstarch
4 cups whipping cream
1 sponge cake
1 cup raspberry jam
1/4 cup orange juice
2 tablespoons raspberry jelly
2 bananas, sliced
2 cups raspberries
2 cups strawberries
1/2 cup whipping cream
1/4 cup toasted sliced almonds

Combine egg yolks, sugar and cornstarch in bowl; mix well. Heat 4 cups whipping cream in saucepan. Add a small amount of hot cream to egg yolk mixture; stir egg yolks into hot cream. Cook until thickened, stirring constantly. Cool to room temperature. Split cake into several layers. Spread 1 cup raspberry jam between layers. Cut cake into thin slices. Line glass bowl with slices. Drizzle with orange juice and 2 tablespoons jelly. Chill in refrigerator. Layer bananas, raspberries and strawberries in prepared bowl. Top with custard. Chill until serving time. Whip 1/2 cup whipping cream in mixer bowl until soft peaks form. Spread over trifle; top with almonds. Yield: 30 servings.

Trifle Tarts: Spoon custard into small tart pans lined with sponge cake or baked pie pastry. Chill until serving time. Cover with fresh raspberries or strawberries, kiwifruit slices, banana slices or any combination of fruit. Serve plain or garnish with sweetened whipped cream and toasted almonds.

Rest of the Meal

Trio Italiano Picnic Salad

1   16-ounce package San Giorgio Trio Italiano
2 cups zesty Italian salad dressing
1/4 cup salad supreme seasoning
2 cups chopped cucumber
2 cups chopped fresh tomatoes
1 cup green bell pepper strips
1 cup chopped celery   1 cup sliced fresh mushrooms
1/2 cup sliced onion

Cook pasta using package directions; drain, rinse with cold water and drain well. Mix salad dressing and seasoning in large bowl. Add pasta; toss gently to mix. Add vegetables; toss gently. Chill for several hours to overnight. Yield: 8 to 10 servings.

Sausage and Zucchini Italiano

1 pound Italian link sausage
1/2 cup chopped onion   2 cloves of garlic, minced
1   28-ounce can tomatoes
1   15-ounce can tomato sauce
2 tablespoons chopped fresh parsley
2 teaspoons basil   1 teaspoon sugar
1/2 teaspoon each salt and oregano
1/4 teaspoon pepper
3 cups uncooked San Giorgio Trio Italiano
2 cups sliced zucchini
Grated Parmesan cheese to taste

Cook sausage in large skillet until brown on all sides. Remove from skillet, cut into thin slices and return to skillet. Add onion and garlic. Sauté until onion is tender but not brown; drain. Add undrained tomatoes, tomato sauce and seasonings. Simmer for 15 minutes, stirring occasionally. Cook pasta using package directions. Add zucchini to sauce. Simmer for 5 to 7 minutes or until zucchini is just tender. Toss pasta with sauce. Serve immediately with Parmesan cheese. Yield: 4 to 5 servings.

Photograph for these recipes is on previous page.

Antipasto

(Italian)

3 to 6 small green bell peppers, chopped
1   10-ounce can chopped mushrooms
1 cup sweet pickle relish
1   4-ounce can chopped pimento
1   7-ounce can solid-pack tuna   6 cloves of garlic, crushed
20 green olives, chopped   20 black olives, chopped
1   20-ounce bottle of catsup
1   10-ounce bottle of chili sauce   1/2 cup vinegar
3 tablespoons corn oil   1/2 cup sugar
Worcestershire sauce to taste
Tabasco sauce to taste   1 bay leaf

Combine green peppers, undrained mushrooms, relish, pimento, tuna, garlic, olives, catsup, chili sauce, vinegar, oil, sugar, Worcestershire sauce, Tabasco sauce and bay leaf in large saucepan. Bring to a boil; reduce heat. Simmer for 10 to 20 minutes or to desired consistency, stirring frequently. Remove bay leaf. Spoon into hot sterilized jars, leaving 1/2 inch headspace. Seal with 2-piece lids. Store in refrigerator for up to 1 year. Yield: 5 pints.

Boursin Cheese Spread

(French)

16 ounces cream cheese, softened
8 ounces margarine, softened
1/4 teaspoon oregano   1/4 teaspoon thyme
1/4 teaspoon marjoram   1/4 teaspoon dillweed
1/4 teaspoon basil   1/4 teaspoon pepper
1/2 teaspoon garlic powder
Coarsely ground pepper

Combine cream cheese, margarine, oregano, thyme, marjoram, dillweed, basil, 1/4 teaspoon pepper and garlic powder in bowl; mix well. Pack into bowl or crock container. Sprinkle coarsely ground pepper over top. Chill, covered, for 24 hours. Serve with assorted crackers or apple slices. Yield: 1 1/4 pounds.

Gouda Bake

*This **French** dish is easy but dazzling. Try a variation using
Brie and puff pastry with a layer of apricot
jam spread over the Brie.*

1 Gouda cheese
1 8-count can crescent rolls
Crackers

Peel red wax covering from cheese. Unroll crescent rolls. Press
together to form square; seal perforations. Wrap roll dough
around cheese. Place on baking sheet. Bake at 350 degrees for 20
minutes or until light brown. May be reheated in microwave. Serve
with crackers. Yield: 6 to 8 servings.

Quick Cheese Fondue

*Tart apples are best or try a variety of dippers for this **French** fondue.
Leftover fondue makes great grilled cheese sandwiches
or spread on toasted English muffins.*

1 10-ounce can Cheddar cheese soup
8 ounces French onion dip
1 cup shredded Cheddar cheese
1/2 teaspoon dry mustard
2 dashes of cayenne pepper
French bread, cut into 1-inch cubes
Apples, cut into bite-sized pieces
Green seedless grapes

Combine cheese soup, onion dip, cheese, mustard and cayenne
pepper in saucepan. Cook over low heat until cheese is melted,
stirring constantly. Pour into chafing dish. Serve with bread cubes,
apples and grapes. Yield: 2½ cups.

Stuffed French Baguette

1 24-inch French bread baguette
8 ounces cream cheese, softened
2 tablespoons lemon juice
2 tablespoons chopped fresh dill
2 green onions, chopped
1 10-ounce package frozen chopped spinach, thawed
4 cups minced ham
1/3 cup chopped pecans
1/2 cup mayonnaise
1 tablespoon Dijon mustard

Cut baguette into halves lengthwise. Scoop out centers, leaving 1/2-inch shells. Wrap loaf tightly with plastic wrap. Combine cream cheese, lemon juice, dill and green onions in medium bowl; mix well. Squeeze spinach dry. Add to cream cheese mixture; mix well. Mix ham, pecans, mayonnaise and mustard in large bowl. Coat inside of shell halves and all cut edges with cheese mixture. Fill with ham mixture. Place halves together; wrap tightly. Refrigerate for 2 to 10 hours before serving. Slice to serve. May substitute 1 teaspoon dillweed for fresh dill. Yield: 30 servings.

Middle Eastern Ham Cornucopias

3 ounces cream cheese, softened
1 tablespoon whipping cream
2 tablespoons chopped crab meat
2 tablespoons finely chopped celery
1/2 cup finely chopped pistachios
4 large, thin slices, cold boiled ham

Combine cream cheese and whipping cream in mixer bowl; mix well. Add crab meat, celery and 1/4 cup pistachios; mix well. Lay ham slices out flat. Spoon 3 tablespoons cream cheese mixture on each. Roll ham slices into cornucopias. Allow some cheese mixture to protrude from open ends. Dip cheese end in remaining chopped pistachios. Serve cold. Yield: 4 servings.

Middle Eastern Hummus

2 15-ounce cans garbanzo beans
1/2 cup toasted sesame seed
6 tablespoons olive oil
6 cloves of garlic
6 tablespoons lemon juice
Salt and pepper to taste
Olive oil
8 pita rounds, cut into quarters

Drain beans, reserving 3/4 cup liquid. Purée beans, sesame seed, 6 tablespoons olive oil, garlic, lemon juice and reserved bean liquid in blender. Place in serving bowl; drizzle with a small amount of olive oil. Serve at room temperature as dip with pita quarters. Yield: 8 servings.

Stuffed Mushrooms

*Try this unusual **Middle Eastern** version—no sausage or crumbs in these stuffed mushrooms.*

1/4 cup butter
8 large mushrooms
1/2 cup chutney
1/4 cup shelled pistachios
1/4 cup chopped walnuts

Melt butter in skillet over medium heat. Peel mushrooms and chop stems. Add mushrooms to skillet. Sauté for 4 minutes, turning once. Remove caps from skillet. Arrange on serving plate. Add chutney, pistachios and walnuts to skillet. Stir-fry for 1 minute. Stuff mushroom caps with stir-fry mixture. Serve hot. Yield: 8 servings.

Polpette di Risotto Italiano

1 vegetable bouillon cube
2 1/2 cups boiling water
1 tablespoon butter   1 cup long grain rice
1/2 cup grated Parmesan cheese
3 egg yolks, slightly beaten
1/2 teaspoon salt   1/4 teaspoon white pepper
2 tablespoons chopped mushrooms
1 tablespoon chopped onion
14   1/4x1x1-inch squares mozzarella cheese
3 egg whites, slightly beaten
1 cup fine dry bread crumbs
Oil for deep frying

Dissolve bouillon cube in boiling water in medium saucepan. Stir in butter and rice. Simmer, covered, for 15 minutes or until rice is tender; drain. Add Parmesan cheese, egg yolks, salt and white pepper; mix well. Stir in mushrooms and onion. Shape 1/4 cup mixture around each piece of mozzarella cheese. Dip into egg whites; coat with bread crumbs. Deep-fry in oil heated to 375 degrees for 5 to 7 minutes or until golden brown. Yield: 14 servings.

Roquefort Diablotins

(French)

1 cup crumbled Roquefort cheese
1/2 cup butter, softened
1/2 cup chopped pecans
1 loaf French bread, sliced

Combine cheese and butter in bowl; mix well. Add pecans; mix well. Toast bread on 1 side on baking sheet. Spread untoasted side with cheese mixture; place on baking sheet. Broil until bubbly. Serve hot. Yield: 24 servings.

Russian Borscht

2 cups salted water
1   10-ounce can beef consommé
3 cups shredded beets
2 carrots, shredded
1 onion, diced
3 cups shredded red cabbage
1   16-ounce can pork and beans
1 tablespoon lemon juice
Sour cream

Bring salted water and consommé to a boil in saucepan. Add beets, carrots and onion. Cook for 20 minutes or until tender. Add cabbage and beans. Simmer, covered, for 15 minutes longer. Stir in lemon juice. Serve hot or chilled, topped with sour cream. Yield: 6 to 8 servings.

Egg Drop Soup

*Quick, easy and a perfect prelude to a **Chinese** banquet.*

3 cups chicken broth
1 teaspoon salt
2 tablespoons cold water
1 tablespoon cornstarch
1 egg, slightly beaten
1 scallion and top, finely chopped

Bring chicken broth to a boil in soup pot. Add salt. Stir in mixture of cold water and cornstarch. Stir a small amount of hot broth into egg; stir egg into hot broth. Cook until clear and slightly thickened, stirring constantly. Garnish with scallion. Yield: 2 to 3 servings.

Chicken soup is a standby in all languages—as comforting as a mother's hug, as therapeutic as a steaming mug or as stimulating as an unexpected taste sensation. This version is zesty, not too hearty and not too light, but a sparkle for tongue and eye.

Greek Lemon Chicken Soup

(English Version)

8 cups chicken broth
1/2 cup lemon juice
1/4 teaspoon pepper
1/2 cup uncooked rice
1 medium carrot, shredded
4 egg yolks, beaten
1 cup chopped cooked chicken
1 lemon, thinly sliced

Bring broth, lemon juice and pepper to a boil in large saucepan. Add rice and carrot; reduce heat. Simmer for 25 minutes. Stir a small amount of soup into beaten egg yolks; stir eggs into soup. Add chicken. Cook until heated through, stirring frequently. Do not boil. Ladle into soup bowls. Garnish with lemon slice.
Yield: 8 servings.

Soupe de Poulet et Citron à la Grecque

(French Translation)

8 tasses de bouillon de volaille
½ tasse de jus de citron
½ cuillerée à café de poivre
½ tasse de riz, non cuit   1 carotte moyenne, râpée
4 jaunes d'œuf, battus   1 tasse de poulet cuit, haché
1 citron, coupé en fines tranches

Mélangez le bouillon, le jus de citron et le poivre dans une grande casserole. Portez à l'ébullition. Ajoutez le riz et la carotte. Mijotez à petit feu pendant 25 minutes. Délayez les jaunes d'œuf avec un peu du liquide chaud. Incorporez les jaunes d'œuf à la soupe, en bien remuant. Ajoutez le poulet. Laissez cuire à feu doux jus'qu'à ce que la soupe soit chaude, en la tournant souvent: ne la laissez pas bouillir. Servez dans des assiettes creuses. Garnissez avec des tranches de citron. Pour 6 personnes.

Griechische Zitronenhühnersuppe

(German Translation)

8 Tassen Hühnerbrühe   ½ Tasse Zitronensaft
¼ Teelöffel Pfeffer   ½ Tasse ungekochten Reis
1 mittlere Karotte, geraspelt
4 Eigelb, geschlagen
1 Tasse kleingeschnittenes gekochtes Huhn
1 Zitrone, dünn aufgeschnitten

Brühe, Zitronensaft und Pfeffer in einem großen Saucentopf zum Kochen bringen. Reis und Karotte hinzufügen; auf kleinere Flamme stellen. 25 Minuten bei kleiner Hitze kochen. Eine kleine Menge Suppe in das geschlagene Eigelb mischen; Eier in die Suppe rühren. Unter häufigem Umrühren aufkochen, jedoch nicht kochen, lassen. In Suppenteller verteilen. Mit Zitronenscheiben verzieren. Für 8 Personen.

Minestra di pollo e limone alla greca

(Italian Translation)

8 tazze brodo di pollo
¹/₂ tazza succo di limone
¹/₄ cucchiaino pepe   ¹/₂ tazza riso crudo
1 carota, tritata   4 rossi di uovo, sbattuti
1 tazza pollo cotto, tritato
1 limone, a fette sottili

Far bollire il brodo, il succo di limone a il pepe in un grande tegame. Aggiungere il riso e la carota e cuocere a fuoco lento 25 minuti. Aggiungere un po' del brodo ai rossi di uovo e girare bene; aggiungere al brodo. Aggiungere il pollo. Cuocere finché caldo, girando frequentemente; non far bollire. Versare in piatti fondi. Mettere sopra fette di limone. Porzioni: 8.

Sopa griega de pollo con limón

(Spanish Translation)

8 tazas de caldo de pollo
¹/₂ taza de jugo de limón
¹/₄ cucharadita de pimienta   ¹/₂ taza de arroz no cocido
1 zanahoria de tamaño medio, rallada
4 yemas de huevo, batidas
1 taza de pollo, cocido y picado
1 limón, cortado en rebanadas delgadas

Hacer hervir el caldo, el jugo de limón y la pimienta en una olla grande. Agregar el arroz y la zanahoria; bajar el fuego. Cocinar a fuego bajo por 25 minutos. Echar un poco de esta sopa a las yemas batidas; echar la mezcla de yemas y sopa en la olla grande. Agregar el pollo. Cocinar hasta que esté bien caliente, revolviéndola frecuentemente: que no se hierva. Servirse en fuentes para sopa. Adornarse con rebanadas de limón.
Rendimiento: 8 porciones.

Spanish Gazpacho

1/4 cup finely chopped onion
1/4 teaspoon minced garlic
1 1/2 cups finely chopped green bell pepper
2 1/2 cups finely chopped peeled tomatoes
2 1/2 teaspoons salt
1/4 teaspoon pepper
1/2 teaspoon honey   1/4 teaspoon paprika
2 tablespoons chopped chives
1/3 cup oil   1/2 cup lemon juice
2 cups tomato juice
1/2 cup shredded cucumber

Combine onion, garlic, green pepper, tomatoes, salt, pepper, honey, paprika and chives in large bowl. Stir in oil, lemon juice and tomato juice. Chill for 2 hours. Stir in cucumber just before serving. Yield: 8 servings.

Minestrone Soup

(Italian)

4 slices bacon, chopped
1 cup chopped onion
1/2 cup chopped celery
3 cloves of garlic, minced   1   10-ounce can beef broth
1 1/2 broth cans water   1 teaspoon basil
1   20-ounce can pork and beans
1   16-ounce can tomatoes, chopped
1/2 cup small macaroni   Salt and pepper to taste
1 cup chopped zucchini
1 cup shredded cabbage

Brown bacon with onion, celery and garlic in soup pot, stirring frequently. Add beef broth, water, basil, pork and beans, undrained tomatoes, macaroni, salt and pepper. Simmer, covered, over low heat for 15 minutes, stirring occasionally. Add zucchini and cabbage. Cook over low heat for 10 to 15 minutes or until vegetables are tender, stirring occasionally. Yield: 4 to 6 servings.

Pasta Fagioli

(Italian)

**1 medium onion, chopped
1 clove of garlic, minced
1 small green bell pepper, chopped
1/4 cup olive oil
4 medium tomatoes, chopped
4 fresh basil leaves   12 Swiss chard leaves
2 cups beef broth
3 cups cooked white beans
Salt and pepper to taste
6 ounces spaghetti, cooked**

Sauté onion, garlic and green pepper in olive oil in 5-quart saucepan for 5 minutes. Add tomatoes and basil. Sauté for 5 minutes. Add chard. Simmer for 5 minutes. Stir in beef broth. Simmer for 5 minutes. Add beans, salt and pepper. Heat to serving temperature. Stir in spaghetti at serving time. Garnish servings with Parmesan cheese. Serve with toasted garlic bread and tossed green salad. Yield: 6 servings.

Cream of Peanut Soup

Don't knock this African dish until you try it.

**1 cup chopped celery
1 cup chopped onion
1/4 cup butter
2 tablespoons flour
8 cups chicken broth
1 cup creamy peanut butter
1 cup half and half**

Sauté celery and onion in butter in large saucepan until tender. Stir in flour. Add chicken broth gradually. Cook until thickened, stirring constantly. Stir in peanut butter. Simmer for 15 minutes. Add half and half. Cook just until heated through; do not boil. Yield: 8 servings.

Pumpkin Soup and Potato Dumplings

(German)

1 small pumpkin, peeled, chopped
Salt and pepper to taste   ¼ cup minced onion
2 tablespoons parsley flakes   ¼ cup butter   4 cups milk
3 pounds potatoes, boiled in skins
2 eggs   1 cup cream of wheat
1 tablespoon salt   2½ to 3 cups flour

Combine pumpkin with salt and pepper to taste and water to cover in saucepan. Cook until tender. Add onion, parsley flakes and butter. Cook for several minutes. Stir in milk. Peel and rice potatoes into bowl. Add eggs, cream of wheat, 1 tablespoon salt and flour; mix and knead to form smooth dough. Drop by teaspoonfuls into boiling water in saucepan. Cook for several minutes or until dumplings rise to top. Add dumplings to soup. Cook until heated through. May shape dumplings into fingers or large balls and serve with sautéed onions and gravy. Yield: 6 servings.

Bouillabaisse d'Epinards

*Hearty **French** spinach soup.*

1 onion, chopped   3 cloves of garlic, crushed
2 teaspoons olive oil   2 pounds spinach
6 small potatoes, peeled, sliced
Fennel, bay leaves and parsley tied in cheesecloth bag
Pinch of saffron   1 quart boiling water
Salt and pepper to taste   6 eggs
6 slices toast   1½ cups shredded Gruyère

Sauté onion and garlic in olive oil in saucepan until tender. Blanch spinach in saucepan; squeeze out water. Add to saucepan. Stir-fry for 5 minutes. Place potatoes, cheesecloth bag and saffron on top. Pour in boiling water; season with salt and pepper. Simmer until potatoes are tender. Break eggs 1 at a time into soup. Poach for 3 to 4 minutes. Remove cheesecloth bag. Ladle broth over toast in bowl. Add slices of potato and 1 egg to each bowl. Serve with shredded cheese. Yield: 6 servings.

Almond Bok Choy

*Don't panic if you don't know bok choy—its other
name is **Chinese** cabbage.*

3 tablespoons sesame seed
6 tablespoons slivered almonds
2   3-ounce packages ramen noodles, broken into pieces
1/2 teaspoon pepper
1 teaspoon garlic powder
1/4 cup vegetable oil   1/4 cup vinegar
1/2 cup sugar
2 tablespoons soy sauce
1 large bunch Napa bok choy, shredded, chilled
1 large bunch green onions, chopped, chilled

Brown sesame seed, almonds, ramen noodles, pepper and garlic powder in oil in skillet; cool. Bring vinegar, sugar and soy
sauce to a boil in saucepan. Let stand until cool. Mix sesame seed
mixture with bok choy and green onions in large bowl. Top with
cooled vinegar mixture; toss well. Yield: 6 servings.

Avocats à la Macedoine

*This **French** vegetable and avocado salad is a feast for the eyes, too.*

1   10-ounce package frozen mixed vegetables
6 avocados
Juice of 2 lemons
2 to 3 tablespoons mayonnaise
Cayenne pepper to taste
1 tomato, sliced

Cook vegetables using package directions for half the time or
until tender-crisp; drain and chill. Cut avocados into halves
lengthwise. Remove seed and scoop out pulp, reserving peel. Cut
pulp into small cubes. Place in bowl; sprinkle with lemon juice. Stir
in vegetables and mayonnaise. Season with cayenne pepper. Spoon
mixture into reserved avocado shells. Garnish with tomato slice.
Yield: 6 servings.

Italian White Bean Salad

Use cannellini beans if you can find them.

10 black olives, pitted
4 anchovy filets, drained
1 tablespoon capers
2 cups canned white beans, rinsed
1/4 cup olive oil
1 clove of garlic, peeled
1 tablespoon lemon juice
2 sprigs of parsley
1/2 teaspoon basil leaves

Slice olives into circles. Cut anchovies into quarters. Combine olives, anchovies, capers and beans in bowl. Add mixture of remaining ingredients; mix lightly. Yield: 4 servings.

Broccoli Tortellini

(Italian)

1   7-ounce package tortellini
1 cup broccoli flowerets
1/2 cup finely chopped fresh parsley
1 tablespoon chopped pimento
1   6-ounce jar artichoke hearts
2 green onions, chopped   2 1/2 teaspoons fresh basil
1/2 teaspoon garlic powder
1/2 cup Italian salad dressing
Sliced black olives
5 or 6 cherry tomatoes, cut into halves
Grated Parmesan cheese

Cook tortellini using package directions; drain. Combine with broccoli, parsley, pimento, undrained artichoke hearts, green onions, basil, garlic powder, salad dressing and black olives in salad bowl; mix well. Chill, covered, for 4 hours to overnight. Add tomatoes and Parmesan cheese just before serving. Yield: 6 servings.

Whether a recipe originated in China, the Middle East, Mediterranean area or South Pacific, you can be sure that the ingredients or manner of preparation or both spotlight its uniqueness. The zing of yogurt and the cool refreshing hint of mint are hallmarks of Arabian and other Middle Eastern delicacies that complement any menu. You may serve this "salad" as an appetizer, a relish or a pretty garnish.

Cucumber Salad Damascus

(English Version)

3 cucumbers, peeled, thinly sliced
1/2 cup yogurt
1 clove of garlic
Salt and pepper to taste
1/4 cup chives
2 tablespoons chopped mint

Place cucumber slices in bowl. Leave yogurt in measuring cup. Peel and crush garlic. Stir garlic and yogurt together. Sprinkle salt and pepper on cucumbers. Refrigerate yogurt mixture and cucumbers separately. Drain cucumbers. Toss cucumbers and yogurt mixture together. Place in salad bowl; sprinkle with chives and mint. Serve cold. Yield: 4 servings.

Salade de Concombres du Moyen Orient

(French Translation)

3 concombres, pelés, coupés en fines tranches
Sel et poivre
1/2 tasse de yaourt
1 gousse d'ail, écrasée
1/2 tasse de ciboulette, hachée
2 cuillerées à soupe de menthe fraîche, hachée

Mettez les concombres dans une jatte; assaisonnez-les avec du sel et du poivre. Mélangez le yaourt et l'ail dans un petit bol. Refroidissez les concombres et le yaourt pendant 1 heure ou jusqu'à l'heure de les servir. Égouttez les concombres. Mélangez-les avec le yaourt. Servez dans une assiette de service. Parsemez avec de la ciboulette et de la menthe. Pour 6 personnes.

Nahöstlicher Gurkensalat

(German Translation)

2 Gurken, geschält, in dünne Scheiben schneiden
Salz und Pfeffer nach Geschmack
1/2 Tasse Joghurt
1 Knoblauchzehe, zerstoßen
1/4 Tasse kleingeschnittenen Schnittlauch
2 Eßlöffel kleingeschnittene frische Minze

Gurken in eine Schüssel geben; mit Salz und Pfeffer bestreuen. Joghurt mit Knoblauch in einer kleinen Schüssel mischen. Gurken und Joghurtmischung eine Stunde lang oder bis zum Servieren in den Kühlschrank stellen. Wasser von Gurken abgießen. Joghurtmischung dazugeben; leicht vermengen. In eine Servierschüssel löffeln. Schnittlauch und Minze darüber verteilen. Für 4 Personen.

Insalata di cetrioli del Medio Oriente

(Italian Translation)

3 cetrioli, sbucciati, a fette sottili
Sale e pepe a piacere
1/2 tazza yogurt
1 spicchio d'aglio, stritolato
1/4 tazza aglio selvatico tritato
2 cucchiai menta fresca tritata

Mettere i cetrioli in una scodella; mettere su un po' di sale e pepe. Mescolare lo yogurt con l'aglio in una piccola scodella. Mettere nel frigo almeno un'ora. Scolare i cetrioli. Aggiungere lo yogurt; mescolare lievemente. Mettere in zuppiera. Aggiungere l'aglio selvatico e la menta. Porzioni: 4.

Ensalada de pepino del Medio Oriente

(Spanish Translation)

3 pepinos pelados, cortados en rebanadas delgadas
sal y pimienta a gusto
1/2 taza de yogurt
1 diente de ajo, molido
1/4 taza de cebolleta picada
2 cucharadas de menta fresca, picada

Echar los pepinos en una fuente, rociar con sal y pimienta. Mezclarse el yogurt y el ajo en otra fuente pequeña. Refrigerar los pepinos, y también la mezcla de yogurt por un mínimo de 1 hora, hasta servirse. Desaguar los pepinos. Echarles la mezcla de yogurt; revolverse. Echarse en una fuente par servirse. Rociar con cebolleta y menta. Rendimiento: 4 porciones.

Chinese Egg Foo Yung Salad

1/2 cup vegetable oil   1/3 cup vinegar
2 tablespoons sugar   1 tablespoon soy sauce
1 head romaine lettuce, torn
1 can bean sprouts, drained
1 can water chestnuts, drained, chopped
2 hard-boiled eggs, sliced
6 slices crisp-fried bacon, crumbled
Salt and pepper to taste

Combine oil, vinegar, sugar and soy sauce in covered jar; shake to mix well. Chill until serving time. Combine lettuce, bean sprouts and water chestnuts in salad bowl; mix well. Add eggs and bacon; mix well. Season with salt and pepper. Add dressing at serving time; toss to mix. Yield: 6 servings.

Greek Salad

1 head leaf lettuce, coarsely chopped
2 tomatoes, chopped
1/2 to 1 green bell pepper, cut into strips
1/2 to 1 yellow bell pepper, cut into strips
8 radishes, sliced   3 stalks celery, sliced
2 carrots, sliced   1 small zucchini, sliced
1 cucumber, sliced   8 mushrooms, sliced
1/4 head red cabbage, shredded
1 onion, sliced into rings
1/3 pound feta cheese, cubed   1 cup oil   1/2 cup vinegar
1/4 teaspoon pepper   1 teaspoon oregano
2 teaspoons garlic salt   2 teaspoons sugar
8 ounces Greek olives
1 red bell pepper, sliced into rings

Combine vegetables and half the feta cheese in serving bowl; toss to mix. Combine oil, vinegar, pepper, oregano, garlic salt and sugar in bowl; mix well. Add to salad; toss to mix. Reserve several olives. Add remaining olives to salad; toss well. Garnish with remaining feta cheese, reserved olives and red pepper rings.
Yield: 8 to 10 servings.

Salade Niçoise

(French)

10 to 12 anchovy filets   ½ cup milk
¾ pound green beans
1   7-ounce can tuna, drained, flaked
2 teaspoons lemon juice   Salt and pepper to taste
½ clove of garlic, crushed   3 tablespoons olive oil
1 small cucumber, peeled, sliced
¼ cup pitted Niçoise olives   3 tomatoes, peeled, quartered

Soak anchovy filets in milk for 30 minutes. Drain and rinse with cold water. Split into halves lengthwise with knife; set aside. Combine green beans with salted water to cover in saucepan. Boil for 8 to 10 minutes or until tender; drain. Spread tuna over bottom of salad bowl. Cover with green beans. Whisk lemon juice with salt, pepper and garlic in small bowl. Whisk in olive oil gradually, beating until sauce is slightly thickened. Pour a small amount of sauce over beans to moisten. Cover with cucumber slices. Drizzle with half the remaining sauce. Arrange anchovy filets in lattice pattern over top, dotting with olives. Arrange tomato wedges around edge of salad bowl. Brush with remaining sauce. Serve at room temperature. May be made up to 8 hours in advance, covered and refrigerated. Yield: 4 servings.

Lebanese Salad

½ head romaine lettuce
2 scallions, trimmed, chopped
1 large tomato, chopped   20 fresh mint leaves, chopped
3 tablespoons olive oil
3 tablespoons white wine vinegar
2 tablespoons wheat germ
⅛ teaspoon salt   Pepper to taste

Tear lettuce into 1-inch pieces. Arrange in salad bowl. Arrange scallions, tomato and mint on lettuce in salad bowl. Sprinkle oil, vinegar and wheat germ over salad. Add salt and pepper to taste. Serve cold. Yield: 2 servings.

Easy German Potato Salad

*Make the salad more colorful by scrubbing the potatoes
well before cooking and leaving the skins on.*

5 pound red potatoes
2 to 3   10-ounce cans cream of mushroom soup
1/2 cup sugar
1/2 cup vinegar
8 ounces sliced bacon, chopped
1/2 cup chopped onion

Boil potatoes in water to cover in large saucepan until tender;
drain. Peel; slice into large salad bowl. Combine soup, sugar
and vinegar in saucepan; mix well. Bring to a boil, stirring constantly. Simmer for 2 to 3 minutes or until smooth, stirring occasionally.
Fry bacon with onion in skillet just until bacon is crisp. Add to
potatoes. Stir in enough soup mixture for desired moistness. Serve
warm or at room temperature. May reduce amount of bacon drippings if desired. Yield: 20 servings.

Irish Potato Salad

2 tablespoons vinegar
1 teaspoon prepared mustard
1/4 cup milk
1 cup mayonnaise
2 teaspoons sugar
1 teaspoon salt
1/4 cup chopped celery
1/4 cup chopped onion
2 cups finely shredded cabbage
1   12-ounce can corned beef, chilled, chopped
1/4 cup chopped dill pickle
4 or 5 medium potatoes, cooked, cooled, chopped

Combine vinegar, mustard, milk, mayonnaise, sugar and salt in
large bowl; mix well. Stir in celery. Add onion, cabbage, corned
beef and dill pickle; mix well. Fold in potatoes gently.
Yield: 6 to 8 servings.

Salade de Tomates à l'Orange

*What an interesting combination from **Italy**—tomato and orange!*
Serve in a bowl lined with deep green lettuce leaves
for the best visual appeal.

4 large ripe tomatoes, cut into eighths
1 tablespoon salt
Freshly ground pepper to taste
¼ cup tarragon wine vinegar
Juice and grated rind of 1 small orange
¼ cup olive oil

Combine tomatoes, salt, pepper, vinegar, orange juice and 2 tablespoons olive oil in bowl, tossing to coat. Chill for 2 to 3 hours. Drain tomatoes before serving. Toss in remaining 2 tablespoons olive oil. Sprinkle with orange rind and serve. Yield: 4 servings.

Green Beans and Onions au Beurre

Tiny green beans fresh from the garden and cooked
*tender-crisp are even better than frozen in this **French** dish.*

1   10-ounce package frozen green beans
1 teaspoon salt
½ cup butter
4 small onions, peeled, thinly sliced
2 tablespoons wine vinegar

Cook green beans with salt using package directions; drain. Melt butter in skillet. Add onions. Cook until tender. Add green beans to skillet. Cook until both green beans and onions begin to brown. Stir in vinegar. Serve hot. Yield: 4 servings.

Haricots Verts Béarnaise

(French)

1 pound green beans, cooked
3 tomatoes, peeled, seeded, chopped
1/2 cup chopped ham
1 clove of garlic, minced
1 tablespoon butter
Salt and pepper to taste

Combine green beans, tomatoes, ham, garlic and butter in saucepan; mix well. Simmer for 5 to 10 minutes or until tomatoes are reduced and mixture is heated through. Yield: 4 servings.

Danish Red Cabbage

Be careful not to cook too long. The cabbage and apples should still have a bit of crunch for contrasting texture.

1/4 cup butter or margarine
1 medium head red cabbage, shredded
2 tablespoons sugar
1/2 cup cider vinegar
2 tart apples, chopped
Salt and pepper to taste
1/2 cup currant jelly

Melt butter in heavy saucepan. Add cabbage, 2 tablespoons sugar, 1/2 cup vinegar, apples, salt and pepper. Cook over low heat until apples are tender-crisp, stirring often. Stir in jelly. Adjust flavor with additional sugar or vinegar for desired sweet and sour taste. Yield: 8 to 10 servings.

Irish Colcannon

4 baking potatoes
4 cups shredded cabbage
3 tablespoons margarine
1/2 cup (about) lukewarm milk
4 green onions, finely chopped
1/2 teaspoon salt   1/2 teaspoon caraway seed
Freshly ground pepper to taste
1/4 cup finely chopped parsley

Scrub potatoes thoroughly. Dry and pierce with fork. Bake at 400 degrees for 1 hour. Cool slightly. Combine cabbage and water to cover in saucepan. Boil, uncovered, for 8 minutes; drain. Cut potatoes down center; scoop out pulp. Set shells aside. Combine potato pulp with margarine in bowl; mash thoroughly. Add enough milk gradually to make creamy consistency. Add cabbage, green onions, salt, caraway seed and pepper; mix well. Fill potato shells with cabbage mixture. Sprinkle each potato with fresh parsley. Yield: 8 servings.

Pierogi Casserole

Polish version of Colcannon.

1 head cabbage, chopped
1 onion, chopped   1 cup margarine
1   16-ounce package lasagna noodles, broken
8 potatoes, cooked, mashed
16 ounces small curd cottage cheese
Salt and pepper to taste
2 tablespoons margarine, softened
Paprika

Sauté cabbage and onion in 1 cup margarine in skillet until onion is transparent. Cook noodles using package directions. Combine cabbage mixture, noodles, potatoes and cottage cheese in large bowl; mix well. Stir in salt and pepper. Spoon into 9x13-inch baking dish. Dot with 2 tablespoons margarine. Sprinkle with paprika. Bake at 325 degrees for 30 minutes. Let stand for 15 minutes before serving. Yield: 6 to 8 servings.

Neapolitan Eggplant

*A typical **Italian** dish but remember that tomatoes came
to Italy from the New World.*

2   28-ounce cans tomatoes
4 cloves of garlic, crushed
2 medium onions, finely chopped
1/4 cup olive oil
2   6-ounce cans tomato paste
2 cups chicken or beef broth
1 tablespoon basil
1 tablespoon oregano
1/2 cup grated Romano cheese
1 tablespoon parsley
3 eggs, beaten
3 tablespoons Romano cheese
Salt and pepper to taste
1 medium unpeeled eggplant, sliced 1/4 inch thick
2 cups flour
1 cup olive oil
Romano cheese
8 ounces shredded mozzarella cheese
Italian bread

Purée tomatoes in blender. Sauté garlic and onions in 1/4 cup olive oil in large saucepan until tender. Add tomato paste and broth. Cook for 5 to 8 minutes, stirring constantly. Add puréed tomatoes, basil, oregano, 1/2 cup Romano cheese and parsley; mix well. Simmer for 30 minutes, stirring occasionally. Combine eggs, 3 tablespoons Romano cheese, salt and pepper in pie plate; mix well. Coat eggplant with mixture of flour, salt and pepper; shake off excess flour. Dip into egg mixture. Brown on both sides in 1 cup olive oil in large skillet. Remove to paper towels to drain. Pour a small amount of sauce in 8x13-inch baking dish. Alternate layers of eggplant, sauce and Romano cheese in prepared dish until all ingredients are used, ending with sauce. Sprinkle with mozzarella cheese. Bake at 350 degrees for 30 minutes or until top is light brown. Serve with Italian bread. Yield: 8 to 10 servings.

German Peas and Kiffels

Another type of dumpling if you are keeping score.

3 eggs, beaten
2 cups flour
Salt and pepper to taste
2 cups fresh or frozen peas
Milk

Mix eggs, flour, salt and pepper in small bowl until a stiff dough is formed. Simmer peas in milk to cover in saucepan until peas are tender. Drop small pieces of dough into peas. Cook until dumplings are cooked through. Yield: 4 servings.

Petits Pois

*The tiniest sweetest peas are best for this **French** favorite.*

1 head romaine lettuce, shredded
3 to 4 cups fresh peas
6 to 8 green onions, sliced
2 teaspoons sugar
4 tablespoons butter
Bouquet garni
1/2 cup water
Salt and pepper to taste
1 tablespoon flour

Combine lettuce, peas, green onions, sugar, 2 tablespoons butter, bouquet garni, water, salt and pepper in heavy saucepan. Simmer, covered, over low heat for 20 to 45 minutes or until peas are tender, stirring occasionally. Discard bouquet garni. Mix remaining butter and flour with fork in small bowl. Add by small pieces to peas, stirring until liquid is thickened. May substitute two 10-ounce packages frozen peas and reduce cooking time to 15 to 20 minutes. Yield: 4 servings.

Peruvian-Style Stuffed Potatoes

8 ounces ground beef
1 small onion, chopped
1 clove of garlic, chopped
1 teaspoon oil   2 tablespoons tomato paste
1 teaspoon chopped parsley
1/4 cup seedless raisins
4 black olives, chopped
1 hard-boiled egg, chopped
1/4 cup white wine   Salt and pepper to taste
4 potatoes, peeled, chopped
1 egg, beaten   1/2 cup flour
Oil for browning

Brown ground beef with onion and garlic in oil in skillet, stir-ring frequently; drain. Stir in tomato paste, parsley, raisins, olives, hard-boiled egg, wine, salt and pepper. Cook potatoes in water to cover in saucepan until tender; drain. Mash until smooth. Add beaten egg, salt and pepper; mix well. Shape into balls; make indentation. Fill with ground beef mixture; shape potato to enclose filling. Coat with flour. Brown in hot oil in skillet. Yield: 6 servings.

Potatoes Romanoff

(Russian)

6 large unpeeled potatoes
2 cups sour cream
1 bunch green onions, chopped
1 1/2 teaspoons salt   1/4 teaspoon pepper
1 1/2 cups shredded Cheddar cheese
Paprika to taste

Cook potatoes in boiling water in saucepan until tender. Peel and shred into large bowl. Stir in sour cream, green onions, salt, pepper and 1 cup cheese. Spoon into greased 2-quart casserole. Top with remaining 1/2 cup cheese and paprika. Chill for several hours. Bake casserole at 350 degrees for 30 minutes or until bubbly. Yield: 8 to 10 servings.

Have you ever given a thought to tomatoes? Did you know that they range from cherry-size to as big as a small melon? The varieties are endless—shapes from round to pear; colors from deep red to yellow; textures from mush to crunch and flavors from sweet to tart. Did you know that tomatoes are really a fruit?

Garlic Cherry Tomatoes

(English Version)

¹/₂ cup butter
1 clove of garlic, peeled, crushed
1 pint cherry tomatoes
Salt and black pepper to taste

Preheat skillet over low heat. Add butter. Cook until melted. Add garlic to butter. Heat but do not brown. Add tomatoes. Heat for 4 minutes over very low flame. Sprinkle with salt and pepper to taste. Serve immediately. Yield: 4 servings.

Petites Tomates à l'Ail

(French Translation)

¹/₂ tasse de beurre
1 gousse d'ail, écrasée
1 pinte de petites tomates
Sel et poivre

Préchauffez la poêle sur un feu doux et faites fondre le beurre. Ajoutez l'ail. Faites-le blondir légèrement. Ajoutez les tomates. Chauffez-les pendant 4 minutes au petit feu en les tournant de temps en temps. Assaisonnez-les avec du sel et du poivre. Servez-les dans une assiette de service garnie de feuilles de cresson ou de laitue. Pour 4 personnes.

Knoblauchkirschtomaten

(German Translation)

¹/₂ Tasse Butter
1 Knoblauchzehe, zerstoßen
1 Pinte Kirschtomaten
Salz und Pfeffer nach Geschmack

Pfanne auf kleiner Flamme vorwärmen. Butter dazufügen. Erhitzen bis Butter geschmolzen. Knoblauch hinzufügen. Sauté, aber nicht bräunen. Tomaten hinzufügen. 4 Minuten lang bei sehr schwacher Hitze kochen, gelegentlich sanft umrühren. Mit Salz und Pfeffer bestreuen. In eine Servierschüssel, die mit Wasserkresse oder Salat ausgelegt ist, löffeln. Für 4 Personen.

Pomodoretti all'aglio

(Italian Translation)

1/2 tazza burro
1 spicchio d'aglio, stritolato
1 pinta pomodoretti
Sale e pepe a piacere

Riscaldare una padella su fuoco lento. Aggiungere il burro e cuocere finché sciolto. Aggiungere aglio e soffriggere ma non rosolare. Aggiungere i pomodoretti. Cuocere a fuoco molto lento 4 minuti, girando ogni tanto. Spargere su il sale e il pepe. Mettere sopra lattuga o crescione in una zuppiera. Porzioni: 4.

Tomates pequeños con ajo

(Spanish Translation)

2 tazas de tomates pequeños
1/2 taza de mantequilla
1 diente de ajo, molido
sal y pimienta a gusto

Calentar una sartén a fuego lento. Echar la mantequilla. Calentar la mantequilla hasta derretirse. Agregarle el ajo a la mantequilla. Saltearse, pero que no se dore. Echar los tomates en la sartén. Calentar por 4 minutos a fuego lentísimo, revolviéndose con cuidado de vez en cuando. Rociar con sal y pimienta. Echar en una fuente, forrada con lechuga o berro, para servirse.
Rendimiento: 4 porciones.

Italian Cheese Risotto

1 cup uncooked rice   2¹/₂ cups water
1 envelope chicken and rice soup mix
1   10-ounce can cream of chicken soup
1   12-ounce can evaporated milk
1   2-ounce jar chopped pimento
1 cup shredded sharp Cheddar cheese

Cook rice, 2¹/₂ cups water and 1 package chicken and rice soup mix in saucepan using package directions. Add remaining ingredients; mix well. Pour into 9x12-inch baking dish. Bake at 350 degrees for 20 minutes. Yield: 12 servings.

Spanish Rice

2 tablespoons olive oil   ¹/₂ cup chopped onion
¹/₂ cup chopped green bell pepper   1¹/₂ cups rice
1¹/₂ cups chicken broth   1¹/₂ cups water   1 tomato, chopped
¹/₂ teaspoon salt   ¹/₄ teaspoon chopped garlic

Heat oil in 2-quart saucepan. Sauté onion and green pepper until tender. Add rice; stir to coat with oil. Add chicken broth, water, tomato, salt and garlic. Bring to a boil; reduce heat. Simmer, covered, for 20 minutes or until all liquid has been absorbed. Yield: 4 servings.

Cranberry Chutney

(English)

1   12-ounce package cranberries   1 cup water
1¹/₂ cups sugar   1 cup orange juice   1 cup chopped walnuts
1 cup chopped celery   1 apple, chopped
1¹/₂ teaspoons grated orange zest   ¹/₄ to ¹/₂ teaspoon ginger
1 cup raisins

Combine cranberries, water and sugar in large saucepan. Bring to a boil. Simmer for 15 minutes, stirring occasionally. Add orange juice, walnuts, celery, apple, orange zest, ginger and raisins; mix well. Remove from heat. Store, covered, in refrigerator. Yield: 2¹/₂ quarts.

Beignets

French doughnuts are breakfast treats worth getting up for.

1 envelope dry yeast   ½ cup lukewarm water
¼ cup shortening
½ cup sugar   1 teaspoon salt
1 cup boiling water
1 cup evaporated milk   2 eggs, beaten
8 cups sifted flour
Oil for deep frying

Dissolve yeast in lukewarm water. Combine shortening, sugar and salt in large bowl. Add boiling water. Cool to lukewarm. Add yeast, evaporated milk, eggs and enough flour to make soft dough; mix well. Knead on floured surface; shape into ball. Place in greased container; cover with greased tight-fitting lid. Heat 5 inches oil to 350 degrees in deep-fryer. Roll portion of dough the size of an orange to ¼-inch thickness on floured surface; cut into 2x3-inch pieces. Deep-fry in hot oil until brown on both sides; drain on paper towels. Dust with confectioners' sugar. Do not allow dough to rise before frying; rising will occur as beignets cook. Yield: 60 servings.

Miniature Blintzes

(Russian)

1   16-ounce loaf white bread
8 ounces cream cheese, softened
½ cup sugar   2 egg yolks
1 cup butter or margarine, softened
1 tablespoon sugar
Cinnamon to taste

Trim bread crusts; roll slices with rolling pin to flatten. Combine cream cheese, ½ cup sugar and egg yolks in bowl; mix well. Spread on bread. Roll each slice as for jelly roll; cut into halves. Blend butter, 1 tablespoon sugar and cinnamon in bowl. Dip rolls into butter mixture; place on baking sheet. Bake at 350 degrees for 4 to 5 minutes or until crisp. Yield: 12 to 16 servings.

Fabulous Italian Breadsticks

For a quicker delight just arrange thinly sliced hot dog
buns on a baking sheet and proceed with the recipe.
Baking will only take 10 minutes or so.

1 loaf frozen bread dough, thawed
3 tablespoons olive oil
1 tablespoon basil
1/2 teaspoon thyme
3 cups shredded mozzarella cheese
Spaghetti sauce

Press out bread dough to fill greased 10x15-inch jelly roll pan. Brush with olive oil. Sprinkle with basil and thyme. Top with cheese. Bake at 350 degrees for 35 to 40 minutes or until light brown. Cut into 1x4-inch strips. Serve with spaghetti sauce. Yield: 4 to 6 servings.

French Breakfast Puffs

1/3 cup shortening
1/2 cup sugar
1 egg
1 1/2 cups flour
1 1/2 teaspoons baking powder
1/2 teaspoon salt
1/4 teaspoon nutmeg
1/2 cup milk
1/2 cup melted margarine
1/2 cup sugar
1 teaspoon cinnamon

Cream shortening, 1/2 cup sugar and egg in bowl until light and fluffy. Add mixture of flour, baking powder, salt and nutmeg alternately with milk. Fill greased muffin cups 2/3 full. Bake at 350 degrees for 20 to 25 minutes or until golden brown. Roll hot muffins in melted margarine; coat with mixture of 1/2 cup sugar and cinnamon. Yield: 15 muffins.

Latin American Buñuelos

2 cups sifted flour   2 tablespoons sugar
1/2 teaspoon baking powder
1/4 teaspoon crushed aniseed
1 teaspoon grated lemon rind
1/2 teaspoon salt   1 egg, slightly beaten
3 tablespoons melted butter or margarine
3 or 4 tablespoons milk   Vegetable oil for frying
2/3 cup honey   1/4 cup butter or margarine

Combine flour, sugar, baking powder, aniseed, lemon rind and salt in large bowl. Stir in egg, 3 tablespoons butter and enough milk to form soft dough. Knead on lightly floured surface for 3 to 5 minutes or until smooth. Let rest for 10 minutes. Divide into 32 equal portions. Roll each into circle on lightly floured surface; edges will be irregular. Stack between waxed paper. Heat 1 inch oil to 375 degrees in heavy skillet. Fry rounds a few at a time for 30 seconds on each side; buñuelos will puff up. Drain on paper towels. Heat honey and 1/4 cup butter in medium saucepan until mixture bubbles for 1 minute. Cool slightly. Drizzle over buñuelos; let stand until set. May freeze unglazed buñuelos or store in airtight container. Reheat at 325 degrees for 1 minute before glazing. Yield: 32 servings.

Orange French Toast

1 1-pound loaf French bread, cut into 1-inch slices
4 eggs   1/4 cup orange juice
1 teaspoon grated orange rind   3/4 cup whipping cream
1/2 teaspoon vanilla extract   1/8 teaspoon nutmeg
Confectioners' sugar   Orange wedges

Place bread slices in 10x15-inch baking pan. Combine eggs, orange juice, orange rind, whipping cream, vanilla and nutmeg in bowl; mix well. Pour over bread, turning slices to coat evenly. Transfer to baking sheet. Bake at 500 degrees for 5 to 7 minutes on each side or until golden brown. Arrange on serving platter. Sprinkle with confectioners' sugar; garnish with orange wedges. Yield: 8 servings.

Mexican-Style Garlic Bread

1 1-pound loaf garlic bread
13 ounces Cheddar cheese, shredded   1 cup mayonnaise
2 tablespoons finely chopped onion
Dash of garlic powder
1¹/₂ green onions with tops, chopped
1 4-ounce can chopped black olives
Chopped jalapeño peppers to taste   ¹/₄ cup melted butter

Split bread into halves lengthwise. Combine cheese, mayonnaise, onion, garlic powder, green onions and olives in bowl; mix well. Add desired amount of jalapeño peppers; mix well. Stir in melted butter. Spread mixture on bread. Place on nonstick baking sheet. Bake at 350 degrees for 15 to 20 minutes or until bubbly. Change oven setting to broil. Broil for 5 minutes or until light brown. Yield: 6 to 8 servings.

Kifles

(Scandanavian)

1 cake compressed yeast
2 cups flour   ¹/₂ cup margarine
2 egg yolks   ¹/₂ cup sour cream
1 cup finely chopped walnuts
¹/₂ cup sugar   1 teaspoon vanilla extract
2 egg whites, stiffly beaten   1 cup confectioners' sugar

Crumble yeast into flour in large bowl. Cut in margarine with pastry blender. Add egg yolks and sour cream; mix well. Knead lightly on floured surface. Divide into 3 portions. Wrap each portion individually in waxed paper. Chill for 1 hour. Mix walnuts, sugar and vanilla in bowl. Fold in stiffly beaten egg whites. Roll 1 portion chilled dough at a time into circle on surface sprinkled with confectioners' sugar. Cut each circle into 8 wedges. Place 1 heaping teaspoon walnut filling on wide end of each wedge. Roll up from wide end. Place seam side down on greased 11x14-inch baking sheet. Bake at 350 degrees for 27 minutes or until golden brown. Remove to wire rack to cool. Store in airtight container. Yield: 24 servings.

Norwegian Lefse

4 cups milk
1/2 cup whipping cream
6 tablespoons butter or margarine
1 teaspoon salt
4 cups flour

Combine milk, whipping cream, butter and salt in 4-quart heavy saucepan. Bring to a full rolling boil almost to top of pan. Remove from heat. Stir in flour quickly. Cool to room temperature. May hasten cooling by dropping large spoonfuls onto tray. Knead on floured surface, adding a small amount of additional flour if needed to form stiff dough. Shape into long roll. Roll out paper-thin with corrugated rolling pin. Cut into shape of round salad plate. Layer on tray. Preheat griddle or lefse baker to 450 degrees. Bake each lefse until light brown on both sides. Serve with butter, sugar and cinnamon. Yield: 9 to 12 servings.

English Muffins Deluxe

*Try substituting toast, bagels, pitas or an assortment
for a truly international experience.*

1/2 cup maple syrup
1/4 teaspoon nutmeg
1 teaspoon grated orange rind
2 tablespoons milk
3 ounces cream cheese, softened
1/4 cup chopped pecans
6 English muffins, split, toasted

Combine maple syrup, nutmeg and orange rind in small bowl; mix well. Combine milk and cream cheese in bowl; beat until soft and creamy. Stir in pecans. Spread cream cheese mixture over toasted side of English muffins; drizzle with syrup mixture. May substitute honey for syrup. Yield: 6 servings.

Pain aux Olives

*This **French** olive bread has the flavor of the Mediterranean.*

2 envelopes active dry yeast
2 pounds flour (mixture of white flour and
1/2 to 1 cup sifted buckwheat flour)
2 cups lukewarm water   2 teaspoons salt
2 tablespoons olive oil   16 ounces black olives, sliced

Stir yeast and 1 cup flour mixture with enough lukewarm water in bowl to make runny batter. Let stand for 1 hour. Warm remaining flour in large bowl in oven. Mix in salt. Make well in center. Pour in yeast mixture, adding enough lukewarm water to form moist dough. Knead for 10 to 12 minutes on lightly floured surface. Let rise, covered with damp towel, in floured bowl until doubled in bulk. Turn out onto floured surface. Punch down to flatten. Sprinkle with olive oil. Knead for 10 minutes. Shape into ball. Let rise, covered, in floured bowl until doubled in bulk. Divide dough into 2 portions; shape each into rectangle. Spread with olives and roll up. Let stand until surface is slightly dry. Brush with water. Place on preheated baking sheet. Bake at 450 degrees for 15 minutes. Reduce temperature to 375 degrees. Bake for 45 minutes longer or until loaves test done. Remove to wire rack to cool. Yield: 2 loaves.

German Apple Pancake

6 eggs   11/2 cups milk   1 teaspoon vanilla extract
1 cup flour   3 tablespoons sugar
1/2 teaspoon salt   1/2 teaspoon cinnamon   1/2 cup butter
3 large tart apples, peeled, sliced
3 tablespoons light brown sugar

Combine eggs, milk and vanilla in mixer bowl; mix well. Add flour, sugar, salt and cinnamon; mix until well blended. Melt butter in 9-inch round baking pan. Place apples over butter. Bake at 425 degrees just until butter begins to sizzle. Pour batter over apples in sizzling hot pan. Sprinkle with brown sugar. Bake for 20 minutes or until pancake is puffed and brown. Serve immediately with favorite toppings. Yield: 6 to 8 servings.

Pancakes, crêpes, waffles, blinis; rolled up, flat, stacked; breakfast, brunch, lunch, dessert; down home, elegant, cosmopolitan—by any name in any guise pancakes are special—plain, sweet, fruit or meat or vegetable filled; hot, cold, flaming; thick, thin...

Swedish Pancakes

(English Version)

5 eggs
2 cups milk
1 cup sifted flour
3/4 teaspoon salt
1/4 cup melted butter
10 tablespoons butter

Beat eggs in mixer bowl until light and fluffy. Beat in milk. Sift in flour and salt; beat until smooth. Add 1/4 cup melted butter; beat until well blended. Prepare pancakes 1 at a time. Melt 1 tablespoon butter in 9 or 10-inch skillet. Add just enough batter to lightly cover bottom of skillet. Fry until golden brown on both sides, turning once. Roll up and sprinkle with confectioners' sugar. Yield: 10 servings.

Crêpes Suédoises

(French Translation)

5 œufs   2 tasses de lait
1 tasse de farine tamisée
³/4 cuillerée à café de sel
¹/4 tasse de beurre fondu
10 cuillerées à soupe de beurre

Battez les œufs dans un bol à mixer avec un fouet électrique. Ajoutez le lait; remuez bien le tout jusqu'à obtenir une préparation onctueuse. Incorporez une ¹/2 tasse de beurre fondu. Préparez les crêpes, une par une. Faites fondre 1 cuillerée à soupe de beurre dans une poêle de 9 à 10 pouces. Ajoutez assez de la pâte pour couvrir le fond de la poêle. Faites cuire jusqu'à ce que la crêpe soit bien dorée sur chaque côté, en la tournant une fois. Repliez les crêpes et saupoudrez-les avec du sucre glace. Pour 10 personnes.

Schwedische Pfannkuchen

(German Translation)

5 Eier   2 Tassen Milch
1 Tasse Mehl, gesiebt
³/4 Teelöffel Salz
¹/4 Tasse Butter, geschmolzen
10 Eßlöffel Butter

Eier in einer Mixschüssel schlagen, bis sie locker und flockig sind. Die Milch dazuschlagen. Mehl hinzusieben und Salz hinzufügen; die Masse schlagen bis sie gut und eben gemischt ist. ¹/4 Tasse geschmolzene Butter hinzufügen; gut schlagen bis alles gut vermischt ist. Jeweils einen Pfannkuchen zubereiten. 1 Eßlöffel Butter in einer etwa 25cm großen Pfanne schmelzen. Gerade genug Teig hineingießen, daß der Boden der Pfanne leicht bedeckt ist. Auf beiden Seiten goldbraun braten, dabei einmal umdrehen. Pfannkuchen aufrollen und mit Konditoreizucker bestreuen.
Für 10 Personen.

Frittelle svedesi

(Italian Translation)

5 uova   2 tazze latte
1 tazza farina
3/4 cucchiaino sale
1/4 tazza burro sciolto
10 cucchiai burro freddo

Sbattere le uova in frullatore finché leggere. Aggiungere il latte. Aggiungere il sale e la farina con lo spargifarina; sbattere finché omogeneo. Aggiungere 1/4 tazza burro sciolto; sbattere finché ben mescolato. Preparare le frittelle una alla volta. Far sciogliere un cucchiaio di burro in una padella di 9 o 10 pollici. Aggiungere solo abbastanza pastella da coprirne il fondo. Friggere finché bruno a tutt'e due i lati. Rotolare e spargere sopra dello zucchero in polvere. Porzioni: 10.

Tortitas suecas

(Spanish Translation)

5 huevos   2 tazas de leche
1 taza de harina cernida
3/4 cucharadita de sal
1/4 taza de mantequilla derretida
10 cucharadas de mantequilla

Batir los huevos en una fuente hasta estarse livianos y esponjados. Agregar la leche y batirse. Agregar cerniéndose la harina y la sal. Batirse hasta quitar los grumos. Agregarse la mantequilla derretida, mezclarse hasta que esté bien mezclado. Prepararse las tortitas una por una. Derretirse una cucharada de mantequilla en una sartén de tamaño de 9 o 10 pulgadas. Echarse apenas suficiente pasta para cubrir el fondo de la sartén. Freírse hasta dorarse tanto el dorso como el verso, dándole una sola vuelta. Arrollarse y rociarse con azúcar. Rendimiento: 10 porciones.

English Currant Scones

1¹/₄ cups currants
2 cups flour
2 teaspoons baking powder
1 teaspoon salt
1 tablespoon sugar
¹/₂ cup shortening   2 eggs, beaten
¹/₂ cup evaporated milk

Rinse and drain currants. Sift flour, baking powder, salt and sugar into bowl. Cut in shortening until crumbly. Add eggs, evaporated milk and currants; mix well. Knead lightly on floured surface. Pat into 8-inch baking pan. Score halfway through into 8 wedges. Bake at 425 degrees for 20 to 25 minutes or until golden brown. Yield: 8 servings.

Orange-Almond Scones

(English)

3 cups flour
4 teaspoons baking powder
¹/₂ teaspoon baking soda
¹/₄ teaspoon salt
¹/₂ cup unsalted butter   ¹/₂ cup sugar
¹/₂ cup slivered almonds
1 tablespoon grated orange rind
1 egg, slightly beaten
¹/₂ cup freshly squeezed orange juice
¹/₄ cup orange yogurt
¹/₄ teaspoon almond extract

Combine flour, baking powder, baking soda and salt in bowl; mix well. Cut in butter until crumbly. Stir in sugar, almonds and orange rind; mix well. Add mixture of egg, orange juice, yogurt and almond extract; mix well. Turn dough onto floured surface. Knead 5 or 6 times. Shape into ball; cut into 8 wedge-shaped sections. Form each section into ball; place on baking sheet. Bake at 375 degrees for 25 minutes. Yield: 8 servings.

Buttermilk Belgian Waffles

It may have been waffles like this that were shaped into cornucopias to become the first ice cream cones.

2 eggs, separated
1¹/₂ cups flour
¹/₄ cup cornstarch
2 teaspoons baking powder
1 teaspoon baking soda
¹/₂ teaspoon salt
6 tablespoons melted shortening
2 cups buttermilk
¹/₂ teaspoon vanilla extract

Beat egg whites in mixer bowl just until stiff peaks form. Beat egg yolks in mixer bowl until light and lemon-colored. Sift flour, cornstarch, baking powder, baking soda and salt together twice. Combine egg yolks, shortening, buttermilk and vanilla in bowl. Add to dry ingredients in large bowl; mix just until moistened. Fold in stiffly beaten egg whites gently. Bake on lightly greased hot Belgian waffle iron until light brown and crisp. Serve with sliced fresh fruit. Yield: 8 servings.

Norwegian Lemon Waffles

5 eggs
¹/₃ cup sugar
¹/₂ teaspoon freshly grated lemon rind
1 cup unbleached flour, sifted
1 cup sour cream
¹/₄ cup melted butter
1 teaspoon lemon juice

Combine eggs with sugar in mixer bowl. Beat for 10 minutes or until light and fluffy. Fold in mixture of lemon rind and flour alternately with sour cream. Stir in butter and lemon juice. Let rest for 10 to 15 minutes. Bake in lightly greased hot waffle iron until steaming stops and waffle is golden brown. Serve hot or cold. Yield: 6 servings.

French Chocolate-Strawberry Cream Torte

1/2 cup Hershey's baking cocoa
1/3 cup boiling water   2 tablespoons butter, softened
1 1/2 teaspoons vanilla extract
6 egg yolks, at room temperature, beaten   1/3 cup sugar
1/3 cup flour   6 egg whites, at room temperature
1/3 cup sugar   1 envelope Knox unflavored gelatin
1/4 cup cold water   1/4 cup milk
3 ounces cream cheese, softened   1/2 cup sugar
2 cups frozen unsweetened strawberries
1/2 cup Hershey's semisweet chocolate chips
2 tablespoons milk

Blend baking cocoa with boiling water in small bowl. Stir in butter and vanilla. Let stand until cool. Beat egg yolks with 1/3 cup sugar in mixer bowl for 3 minutes. Beat in chocolate mixture. Fold in flour. Beat egg whites in mixer bowl until foamy. Add 1/3 cup sugar gradually, beating until stiff peaks form. Fold a small amount of stiffly beaten egg whites into chocolate mixture; fold chocolate mixture into egg whites. Spread batter evenly in greased 10x15-inch cake pan lined with greased waxed paper. Bake at 350 degrees for 12 minutes. Invert onto waxed paper-lined baking sheet on wire rack. Remove cake pan and waxed paper. Cool for 10 minutes. Invert onto wire rack to cool completely. Cut into thirds; trim edges so that layers will fit into 5x9-inch loaf pan. Soften gelatin in cold water in small saucepan. Heat until dissolved, stirring constantly. Stir in 1/4 cup milk. Bring just to the boiling point. Pour into blender container. Add cream cheese; process until smooth, adding 1/2 cup sugar gradually. Add frozen strawberries gradually, processing constantly. Pour into bowl. Chill for 20 minutes. Alternate cake layers and strawberry mixture in 5x9-inch loaf pan sprayed with nonstick cooking spray, ending with cake. Chill, covered, for 8 hours or longer. Loosen from sides of pan with wet metal spatula. Unmold onto serving plate. Heat chocolate chips and 2 tablespoons milk in small saucepan over low heat, stirring constantly. Drizzle over layers. Garnish with sliced strawberries. Yield: 8 servings.

Photograph for this recipe is on the cover.

Silk Chocolate with Citrus Sauce

(French)

1 envelope Knox unflavored gelatin
¹/₂ cup cold water   ³/₄ cup sugar
¹/₂ cup Hershey's baking cocoa
1 teaspoon vanilla extract
1 cup light cream
1 cup whipping cream, whipped
Sliced fresh fruit
Citrus Sauce

Soften gelatin in cold water in small saucepan. Heat over low heat until dissolved, stirring constantly. Mix sugar with baking cocoa. Stir into gelatin mixture gradually. Cook until dissolved, stirring constantly. Mix with vanilla and light cream in large bowl. Chill for 30 minutes or until mixture mounds when dropped from spoon. Fold in whipped cream. Spoon into dessert dishes. Chill until set. Top with sliced fresh fruit and Citrus Sauce. Yield: 8 servings.

Citrus Sauce

¹/₄ cup sugar
1¹/₂ teaspoons cornstarch
Salt to taste   ¹/₃ cup orange juice
2 tablespoons water
1 tablespoon lemon juice
1 teaspoon butter
¹/₄ teaspoon grated orange rind
2 tablespoons sour cream

Combine sugar, cornstarch and salt in small saucepan. Blend in orange juice, water and lemon juice. Bring to a boil over medium heat, stirring constantly. Simmer for 3 minutes, stirring constantly; remove from heat. Stir in butter and orange rind. Cool. Blend in sour cream just before serving. Yield: ¹/₂ cup.

Photograph for these recipes is on the cover.

Chocolate Banana Mousse Cake

(French)

**2 cups graham cracker crumbs   1/4 cup Hershey's baking cocoa
1/4 cup sugar   1/2 cup melted butter
1 envelope Knox unflavored gelatin   1/2 cup cold water
16 ounces cream cheese, softened   1 1/2 cups sugar
1 cup mashed bananas   1/3 cup Hershey's baking cocoa
2 teaspoons vanilla extract   1 cup whipping cream, whipped**

Combine crumbs, 1/4 cup baking cocoa, 1/4 cup sugar and melted butter in bowl; mix well. Press over bottom and side of 9-inch springform pan. Bake at 350 degrees for 10 minutes. Cool completely. Soften gelatin in cold water in small saucepan. Heat until dissolved, stirring constantly. Beat cream cheese with 1 1/2 cups sugar in mixer bowl until light and fluffy. Add bananas, 1/3 cup baking cocoa and vanilla; beat until smooth. Beat in gelatin mixture gradually. Fold in whipped cream. Pour into prepared springform pan. Chill for 8 hours or longer. Place on serving plate; remove side of pan. Garnish with sliced bananas. Yield: 12 servings.

Chocolate Amaretto Cheesecake

(French)

**1 cup coconut cookie crumbs   1/4 cup ground almonds
1/4 cup butter, softened   1 envelope Knox unflavored gelatin
1/4 cup cold water   16 ounces soft cream cheese   1 cup sugar
1/2 cup Hershey's baking cocoa   3/4 teaspoon almond extract
1 teaspoon vanilla extract   1 cup whipping cream, whipped**

Mix crumbs, almonds and butter in bowl. Press over bottom of 9-inch springform pan. Bake at 350 degrees for 10 minutes. Cool completely. Soften gelatin in cold water in small saucepan. Heat until gelatin is dissolved, stirring constantly. Beat cream cheese with sugar in mixer bowl until light and fluffy. Add baking cocoa and flavorings; beat until smooth. Beat in gelatin mixture gradually. Fold in whipped cream. Pour into prepared springform pan. Chill until firm. Place on serving plate; remove side of pan. Garnish with sweetened whipped cream and chocolate curls. Yield: 12 servings.

Photograph for these recipes is on the cover.

Menus International

German Oktoberfest

Celebrate Oktoberfest in the manner of a harvest thanksgiving. Merrymaking should be the order of the day! With an "oom pah pah" of a polka band for atmosphere and a frosty mug of root beer for everyone, clear the area for circulating, dancing, singing and fun, fun, fun! Good eating!

German Sauerbraten Meatballs, page 24, or
Oktoberfest German Sauerkraut, page 35
Easy German Potato Salad, page 126
Black Forest Chocolate Cheesecake, page 66, or
German Apple Pancake, page 142

Italian Classic Dinner

Use red, green and white (the colors in the Italian flag) to set a Mediterranean mood. Add some big yellow flowers for a hint of the sun and some dripping candles for a touch of the romantic. Provide some olives and a dish of freshly grated Parmesan or Romano cheese to pass. Select the freshest fruit available for dessert and don't forget a few figs.

Antipasto, page 107
Italian Veal Parmigiana, page 41, or
Fettucini Alfredo Florentine, page 64
Broccoli Tortellini, page 120
Fabulous Italian Breadsticks, page 138
Italian Anise Cookies, page 67, and
Fresh Fruit

Menus International

Greek Toga Party

*H*ave an instant costume party. Greet guests with a collection of not-too-large and not-too-small sheets (flat—not fitted ones) and provide some pins for instant toga draping. Be sure to provide dishes of olives, almonds and assorted grapes cut into small clusters for nibbling before, during and after dinner. A punch of equal parts lemonade and grape juice served in a heavy goblets will lend a touch of authenticity. Add a musical background from Zorba the Greek.

Greek Lemon Chicken Soup, page 113
Moussaka, page 27, or
Greek Seafood Baklava, page 56
Greek Salad, 124
Grecian Galatobourika, page 96

Far East Delight

*S*et the coffee table instead of the dining table and have guests remove shoes before sitting on pillows around the table. Bamboo placemats and chop sticks complete the decor. Serve with soy sauce and hot mustard sauce condiments.

Egg Drop Soup, page 112
Kung Pao Pork, page 34, or
Szechwan Chicken and Cashews, page 50
Chinese Hot and Sour Spareribs, page 40
Cantonese-Style Egg Foo Yong, page 59
Almond Bok Choy, 119
Steamed Rice   Fortune Cookies   Hot Tea

Menus International

Festive Mexican Dinner

Use your brightest colors of dinnerware and napkins. Make a centerpiece of large brilliant paper flowers or cluster a few small cactus plants on a tray covered with sand. Add a huge bowl of tortilla chips and keep the ice water at the ready.

Spanish Gazpacho, page 116

Mexican Chicken Fajitas, page 46, with

Fresh Salsa, page 46, and Guacamole, page 47

Mexican Chilies Rellenos, page 57

Spanish Rice, page 136

Fried Mexican Ice Cream, page 96, or

Mexican Capirotada, page 99

Vive la France Dessert Crêpe Party

Make some additional crêpes in advance or buy them from the frozen food case or your friendly neighborhood French bakery. Provide some additional fillings—sweetened whipped cream, several flavors of ice cream and/or creamy pudding, even canned pie filling or fresh fruit thinly sliced and lightly sweetened. Allow guests to pick, choose and build their own creations (with the admonition that eating follows building). An assortment of flavored instant coffees will complement the desserts.

French Almond Crêpes, page 92

Chocolate Chocolate Crêpes, page 93

Viennese Crêpes, page 94

Recipe Index by Categories

Recipe Index by Country

Index of Translated Recipes